CW00435568

Also by Matthew Woodward:

Trans-Siberian Adventures
A Bridge Even Further
The Railway to Heaven

Silver Streak
*An adventure where the railroad
and Hollywood collide*
Matthew Woodward

LANNA HALL PUBLISHING

This book is dedicated to John.

John works as an attendant in a busy dining car on the Sunset Limited between New Orleans and Los Angeles. He serves passengers freshly cooked meals three times each day, always with a big smile. But John doesn't work in the usual sort of catering business. He has a greater calling. John's job is looking after his passengers in the proud traditions of service on the American railroad. He sums up the spirit of many of the Amtrak employees who work on long-range rail routes across America. In difficult situations I now ask myself 'What would John do?' The answer is always the same. With his big warm smile, he'd ask what's needed and offer to help. Amtrak is a business under much pressure to change – I hope that it doesn't lose sight of what its greatest asset is. This book is dedicated to John and all his colleagues who like him work tirelessly on Amtrak long-distance trains.

'Life moves pretty fast. If you don't stop and look around once in a while, you could miss it.'

'Ferris Bueller's Day Off', John Hughes (1986)

Contents

Introduction

The original Silver Streak was known as the Silver Streak Zephyr, a lightweight streamliner that began running from Lincoln, Nebraska, to Kansas City, Missouri, in 1940. A sister service, the Pioneer Zephyr, became famous by making a daily 'dawn to dusk dash' from Denver to Chicago. In 1934 Tommy Atkins directed a film based on the Pioneer Zephyr, titling it *Silver Streak*. The plot is strangely relevant to the world we live in today: it was about a mercy run by a train carrying urgently needed medical supplies during a rampant polio epidemic.

When Amtrak took control of American passenger trains in the early 1970s it inherited rolling stock dating back to the 1940s. It placed an order for a new type of carriage partly based on the hi-level double deck cars of the Santa Fe Railway and its famous trains like the Super Chief with its big domed lounge carriages and lavish dining cars. Amtrak's advertising agency, Needham, Harper & Steers, came up with the new name – and the Superliner was born.

In 1976 Arthur Hiller made a rather different film of the same name, but in the comedy action genre. This time the setting was the route from Los Angeles to Chicago that is now served by The Southwest Chief. Amtrak would not co-operate in the making of the movie, as the plot involved a huge train crash at Chicago Union Station, so the railroad sequences were mostly shot using specially disguised trains on the Canadian Pacific Railway. *Silver Streak* hasn't stood the test of time too well. It portrays race and gender stereotypes that feel awkward today but were very normal on screen in the 1970s. The plot is also at times totally baffling. But if you try and overlook these shortcomings, it's an otherwise funny and carefree film. Gene Wilder is in his element, and once Richard Pryor finally appears, they make a great comedic double act.

Travel by train is pretty unfashionable in many parts of the United States in current times. Americans no longer see the railroad in the way that they did in the period when streamliners like the original Silver Streak were *the* way to travel. Long-distance train travel might not be as fast as an airplane, as cheap as a bus or as convenient as a car – but it offers an amazing way to see the landscapes, meet the people and discover places you would not otherwise visit – or perhaps even know existed. But beyond the functionality of travel, to me there is something deeply exciting about sitting in the Union Station Metropolitan Lounge in LA waiting to board a train that will arrive 2265 miles down the line in Chicago nearly two days later. Once on board you will have your own room, and there will be a bar, a dining car and an observation lounge. Yes please!

After writing extensively about life on the rails in Central Asia I realised that I needed a new railway to fall in love with. I completed a reconnaissance trip across the US by train in 2017 and realised straight away that I had a whole new *continent* to fall in love with. I had originally planned to make two further trips to gain material for this book. I completed the first in February 2020, returning to my home in England just days before the lockdown as Covid-19 took hold of our lives. In my shoulder bag were two thick notebooks full of more scribblings than I have ever made on any past adventure.

But I also wanted to do something slightly different in this book – to share my interest in cinema and see what happened in the world where trains and films collide, sometimes literally.

Matthew Woodward
Chichester, West Sussex, 2020.

Silver Streak

Lost in Translation

The first-time Amtrak traveller might be surprised by the on-board language, which is usually both polite and slightly formal. Tickets might be inspected 'presently' and the dining car might open 'momentarily'. But usually nothing much will go wrong if you accidentally ask for directions to your compartment (it's a room or roomette) or the buffet car (it's a dining car), other than getting a blank look and the curt response 'Sir, I don't understand what you are saying.'

The train language of the rest of the world has only had a limited chance to interbreed with North America, leaving it with its own unique rail dialect. Before embarking on a rail adventure there, it can be helpful to learn the meaning of a few of these words. Sometimes several words describe the same thing, and it's useful to know which words are interchangeable.

So, if you don't happen to know the difference between a thunder pumpkin and a toaster, a double spot and a dorm car, or a brakeman and a bumper, then please consult the 'Learn to Speak Amtrak' chapter at the end of the book. It's hugely satisfying to be able to use some of the less well known words at the right moment!

Chapter One
The Junior Boys Film Club

Life at my boarding school in the late 1970s was still pretty traditional. Not quite Tom Brown's Schooldays, but still a life saturated with strange customs, long and muddy cross-country runs and unusual leisure activities. I lived in a dormitory with 30 other boys, sat at a desk with a built-in ink pot covered with Victorian graffiti carved under the lid, and did my best not to get too badly beaten up at various sports on the huge playing fields. I wasn't very good at anything and had much catching up to do. It was very different from my life in the outside world.

Day-to-day pleasures at school were simple. I spent my free time learning how not to crash too painfully on my budget skateboard, violently smashing conkers on long bootlaces, and playing some reasonable table tennis. They say routines are good for you, and nowhere has more of a routine than a British boarding school. Bells to warn about more important bells coming shortly, endless roll calls and carefully scheduled activities to keep you out of any mischief. But the tone of the place always softened and slowed down at the weekend. After games on a Saturday afternoon you were left with that glorious anticipation that other than an enforced church service on Sunday morning, you could choose what to do with your time for more than 24 hours. Knowing you had a period of respite from the regime left you with a warm and blissful feeling and something you had been longing for all week.

But perhaps the thing we looked forward to more than anything else at the weekend was the movie that would be shown in the junior common room after dinner on Saturday evening. I think dinner might have been called tea back then. I'm not talking about something on the television here, but a film on a large ancient projector with great reels of celluloid film. A single speaker at the front of the room and a pull-down screen on a tripod provided a huge amount of low-tech excitement and escapism. We had the Colonel to thank for our movies, a slightly frightening, well-built man with a bald head, bushy ginger eyebrows and a love of good war films. Or of a good war, full stop. The Colonel was a geography teacher, but that was really just a cover story for his other job as the officer commanding the school cadet force or, as he saw it, his own private army. In later years, when I had been recruited into his outfit, I would learn to love his ways. He never cursed or swore. In the event of a minor catastrophe he would just slowly and carefully utter the words 'Oh dear!' in his booming voice. If you were guilty of reading your map coordinates wrongly or, god forbid, losing an item of kit, you would hope the ground would open up beneath you. For added effect if things were more serious, he would combine this phrase with smashing his clenched fist into the palm of his other hand. The effect was more withering than the Bren gun from the school armoury set to fully automatic.

The Colonel's study was on the top floor of our wing of the school, a small room with a large wooden desk behind which stood a range of artillery shells to hold his burgeoning collection of umbrellas, spears and canes. If you were brave or insane enough to secretly search for it, somewhere on his desk in a manila folder, you would have found a list of the current films available from his specialist supplier. But the selection of these movies wasn't something we had any input into. I imagine that the Colonel went to see the headmaster once a term to propose which films he planned to screen. It must have been an interesting meeting and a distraction from more mundane discussions about setting sports fixtures or issuing demerits. Selection would have been based on a carefully developed formula of just the right amount of blood and guts, lots of heroics and a good measure of British stiff upper lip. Sex was frowned upon but tolerated if essential in an otherwise suitable film. Any religious humour was absolutely off the table. In a Venn diagram the films had to fit into the narrow overlap of being character-building, adventurous, and demonstrating the imagined values of future leaders of men.

There didn't seem to be much concern about film certification and, looking back, some of the choices would have been more appropriate to a more mature audience. And that was the problem: we weren't mature at all, and the Colonel would easily get upset by our behaviour – but we were, after all, schoolboys. When someone blew a wolf whistle at the moment when Suzan Farmer gets undressed in *633 Squadron*, the film was stopped and the culprit ejected. The rumour was that the guilty boy was placed in detention until he had learned the name and location of every single Scottish island from a large map on the wall. When we cheered at the scene in *The Wild Geese* where Hardy Kruger takes out the prison camp guards with a special high-power crossbow, the film was cancelled and we had to revert to a game of round-the-table ping pong until bed time.

Unusually, the film advertised on one particular night wasn't a war film and I would not have placed it in the right part of the Venn diagram, but the poster looked highly promising. It had an illustration of a big red and white striped rail locomotive smashing through the walls of a station. There were hand-drawn images of the main actors, who I mostly didn't recognise. I had never seen a film starring Richard Pryor or Gene Wilder before. I didn't have a clue who Patrick McGoohan was either, as *The Prisoner* was deemed far too subversive for children at the time. *Silver Streak* was originally released in 1976 but this copy of the film had taken a couple of years to filter down to the schools, prisons and oil rigs market.

I reached a deal with another boy in my house that we would take our tea in shifts so that our coveted seats in the exact middle of the room could be defended from bigger boys and latecomers. Tonight was too important to risk relying on items of tied-up sports kit to reserve our chairs. Rations were purchased from the tuck shop in case the wait might become too much for us – large bottles of cream soda and several bags of the newly launched pickled onion version of Monster Munch, the 'go-to' crisp of the time.

As the room filled it up it quickly became overheated. Excited small talk grew into a cacophony. Then finally it was time. The Colonel put his pipe in his pocket, made some final adjustments to some of the knobs and switches on the projector and pressed the play button. Applause quickly died down the as film began to roll. A grainy 10 … 9 …. 8 … 7 … 6 … 5 … 4 … 3 … 2 … 1 flickered on the screen in front of us. No Pearl & Dean adverts, no government films about the dangers of playing on railway lines, just straight into the main event. The voiceover on the trailer before the film declared, 'By plane, by train, by the edge of your seat, it's the most hilarious suspense ride of your life. Nothing can stop

Silver Streak!'

On the surface of it, the plot of *Silver Streak* is fairly straightforward, but I find it unnecessary to my enjoyment of the film. This is a spoiler alert, but it's a consistent theme of this book, and I feel that I have to share it with you. Gene Wilder plays a character called George Caldwell, a book editor travelling from Los Angeles to Chicago by train. Witnessing a murder, he becomes embroiled in a fight with some baddies led by Patrick McGoohan who plays Roger Devereau, a corrupt art dealer. Caldwell romances Hilly Burns, Devereau's beautiful assistant, before getting involved with Grover Muldoon, an escaped criminal. Caldwell gets thrown off the train on more than one occasion, and after a series of gunfights he helps the FBI take back control of the train, uncoupling the locomotive from the carriages before it ploughs through Chicago's Union Station. The carriages slow down safely and our heroes come out of their adventure just fine. The underlying plot has been complicated by the discovery of the 'Rembrandt letters', but let's not worry too much about this right now. The producer, Alan Ladd Junior, said: 'It was like the old Laurel and Hardy comedies. The hero is Laurel, he falls off the train, stumbles about, makes a fool of himself, but still gets the pretty girl.'

We watched the film with a sense of wonder and excitement at what it must be like to travel on board such a huge silver train, one that had private cabins and a dining car. Not a British Rail buffet with little more than a stale pork pie, but a real restaurant where a uniformed waiter served you at your table. Outside, the scenery was breathtaking: America as I knew it from wild west films. One day, I thought, I want to take a train like that. I just didn't know how long I was going to have to wait.

Silver Streak

Chapter Two
Groundhog Day

The immigration queue at JFK is predictable in its length, snaking backwards and forwards towards the gates where officers will decide who is going to be admitted to the United States today. A sign estimates the length of the wait, but it's hopelessly optimistic. Every few minutes I pass the same bored people in the queue as we dogleg forward in opposite directions, each time a few metres closer to freedom. Everyone has the same downtrodden look of transatlantic tiredness, but fused with the minor excitement of being at the border. You have to be pretty thick-skinned not to feel slightly guilty about going through border control, even if you have a clean passport and haven't ever had a parking ticket. Just the act of trying to look innocent can make you feel guilty. Will the FBI be onto my failure to return a library book in 1982 or maybe that speeding fine in 1998? I try to concentrate on my book and push my bag forwards every now and then as I progress up the queue to a position that feels like I might get through in the next hour. I have a Buddhist approach to queuing. By recognising that the length of my wait is out of my control I no longer feel stressed about it. In the footsteps of T.E. Lawrence, the trick is to not *mind* if you might be here for an hour or even a day.

The officer at the gate I am directed to is a young woman who looks Chinese. She gives me a brief glance before beginning to examine my passport. I never know where to look when my passport is being inspected. I imagine that if you stare at the officer you might look a bit creepy, but by looking into the distance you appear that you might be hiding something. Instead I tried to focus on the desk in front. Peering over the fingerprint machine I can also see that she's wearing a trusty Glock pistol in a tactical holster, which looks enormous on her tiny waist. I'm a little bit worried about the signals my passport might send, the moment that she will see the multitude of visas to countries not in favour with her incumbent president's foreign policy. Not really dodgy countries, but places where wars have been fought in previous generations.

'What's the purpose of your visit to the United States?' she asks without looking up. Well at least I can answer *that* in a straightforward way. 'I'm here to travel on your trains,' I tell her, slightly too gushingly. 'I'm going right across America, coast to coast and back again.' Most Americans have given up on the train, so my story must sound a bit odd. 'Have you done that before?' she asks, as if to check if I'm mad, or if I'm making a big mistake if I'm not. Then she asks me why I'm travelling alone. 'Meeting any friends?' she asks. 'No, I like to travel by myself on trains – it's much more fun,' I tell her. I sense that her finger must be hovering on a hidden panic button. Code red: call the medics with the straitjacket and the trolley with the gimp mask to Gate 55.

Whatever she's doing takes some time and I fear that her computer seems to be saying 'no' or selecting me for a further attention. 'Have you ever had a problem getting into the United States before?' she asks. This doesn't sound good. I wish I had returned that library book on time now. But after some more checks on the computer she proceeds to take my fingerprints before turning her attention back to some of the trips recorded in my passport. 'How far is your railroad trip going to be?' she asks. I haven't prepared for a difficult question like that, so I tell her I that have no idea. 'About as far as from London to Baghdad, maybe?' she asks whilst poring over the pages of odd-looking visas. 'Maybe,' I tell her, adding quickly, 'but I haven't been to Iraq.' Was that a trick question? Have I passed, or will I get taken away for further questioning? But she seems happy enough, and I think that at that moment that she has decided that, mad or not, I'm suitable to be admitted to the land of the free. 'Amtrak. You've got to love them,' she says, returning my little red book to me with a nice smile. I nod politely and walk through to the baggage reclaim without looking back or too relieved. That would definitely look suspicious.

In the reclaim hall the bags are already off the carousel in a line and waiting for those who have made it in. I pick up a cab for the ride into Manhattan. In the back of an overworked Toyota minivan with limited remaining suspension and velour seats so dirty that they could be used to teach biology, my mind wanders. Here I am, about to kick off an adventure which will probably involve more rail mileage in just a month than the average American takes in an entire lifetime. After several years travelling in Russia and other parts of Asia by train I am about to experience something completely different. Here in the United States, the only thing in common with many of the countries I have visited up until now is the gauge of the track. My hope for this trip had been that I would be able to meet people and talk in the same language to find out about their lives. The challenge that I faced in the Far East had always been just trying to find a few words in common with the people I met along the way. I had the suspicion that the problem here would be getting people to stop talking. Only time would tell.

The very nature of the train was also going to be quite different. Rather than sharing a compartment typical across much of Europe and Asia, I would have my own room most of the time. The windows would be sealed shut, but that shouldn't be a problem as the trains have good air conditioning. There would be a lot more space than I was used to. As well as the dining car there would often be an observation lounge with a café, so I would have plenty of places to hang out in the double-decker carriages known as Superliners. It all sounded rather exciting and fed right into my Silver Streak fantasy.

Inexperienced at organising a train trip in this part of the world, I had discovered that you can't just turn up and buy a ticket. Well you can, but not for a sleeper. But I need to stop right there and immediately change dialect. It's a railroad here, and sleepers are not really sleepers, but dorm cars with rooms and roomettes. The sooner that I stop using words like 'compartment' and 'cabin' the better. Anyway, you can't just turn up and buy a ticket for a room. Despite attitudes to train travel here, roomettes sell out months in advance and are priced like airline tickets so that the later you leave your booking, the more expensive it becomes. But all the long-distance trains also have coach class, something similar to a first-class seat on a European train or an old-fashioned first-class seat on a plane.

Using a good agent in the UK I'd managed to make reservations to travel on some glamorous-sounding trains with names like the Southwest Chief and the Sunset Limited. I don't understand why all trains don't have names like these. In Britain and much of Europe, people used to running airlines have mostly defaulted to giving trains boring and sterile numbers, whereas names are part of the history and connect you more with the journey. Which would you rather travel on – the Orient Express or the EN262? The Flying Scotsman or the 05.40 from Edinburgh Waverley? What a missed marketing opportunity!

Back at home in England, in the study that I call the Engine Shed, I had printed out a large map of the Amtrak network and devised a practicable route. A yellow marker pen crossed the country, looping south and west before returning back to the north-east, and a route marked in green showed the parts that I had already completed on an earlier trip. An orange pen suggested another route for a future trip, but it was too much to cover both the orange and yellow routes on a single trip. I feared that if I tried to do that I would run out of money, or worse still risk losing my rail mojo. So ahead of me on this trip was the yellow route. Starting from New York, I would travel to Chicago before heading south to the Gulf of Mexico. From there I would work my way westwards to Los Angeles and the Pacific Ocean, and then back east to Chicago on the route of the Silver Streak. This map is now in my bag, along with all my rail adventure paraphernalia – a hardback copy of the 1879 Appleton's General Guide to the United States and Canada, an inflatable globe, and copies of the train timetables marked up with notes of things to see and do along the way.

The cab driver finds my little hotel in Rose Hill, and

once checked in I do my best to settle into a room that is no more than a foot bigger than the edges of the bed. I should have remembered that rooms in NYC are always on the small size, but after realising there is not even enough space for me to open my suitcase, I head back down to reception and ask for their thoughts about this. The duty manager takes pity on me and offers to switch me to a different room, the benefit of which is that I can actually put a suitcase down on the floor. The only downside is that the bathroom is miniaturised to compensate. The wash basin is partly in the shower and partly over the toilet. Some flexibility is going to be needed during my ablutions, but I tell myself that this is good training for life on the rails.

The woman who cuts my replacement key has an accent I can't quite place. I guess it's Eastern European. She tells me that today is Groundhog Day, and says something about the weather that I can't quite understand. It turns out that the groundhog is a badger-like weather-forecasting creature: if it sees its own shadow when emerging from hibernation, it retreats and hides, knowing that the clear – and cold – weather means spring is going to be delayed by a few weeks. Apparently, you can eat a groundhog, but it needs a lot of marinating. I remember seeing the 1993 film of the same name with Bill Murray and Andie MacDowell, and only hope that I'm not going to keep waking up in impossibly small hotel bedroom rooms for the next few days.

Walking down 3rd Avenue I also quickly discovered that Groundhog Day also means that today is an unofficial holiday in America for another reason – it's Super Bowl Sunday. Bars and restaurants are heaving with crowds of people looking for a view of the big screen. Industrial quantities of pizza and chicken wings are being served with beer. Whether you like American football or not, this seems to be something of a tradition, one that I'm more than happy to join in with. I find a little Irish bar that I like the look of called Molly's, and inherit the only available stool at the bar from a man who's just leaving. I have to level with you that I don't understand American football, so I decide that I will just cheer randomly for the underdogs for the next couple of hours. The Kansas City Chiefs are playing the San Francisco 49ers, and as the Chiefs are favourite to win I decide to support the 49ers. Opinion on my loyalty is split at the bar. The Chiefs haven't won for 50 years, and I sense they're the more popular team in these parts. The rules baffle me, and some of my shouts of encouragement might come at the wrong moments or in support of the wrong team. I can tell this when the man next to me with a huge Father Christmas beard who chooses to speak only Hebrew looks disdainfully at me and throws his hands into the air.

There are no groundhogs on the menu, so I munch my way through several plates of spicy wings. I can now see why America gets through 1.25 billion chicken wings on this day each year. The first half ends up a tie, but in the third quarter the Chiefs forge ahead and the game ends up a 31–20 victory to Kansas City. To my untrained eye there seems like a lot of shouting and coach decision-making in exchange for little activity on the pitch, but the bartender explains that's how it works. But there is the feeling of a real sense of occasion, and I am probably the only person in the room having to pretend to understand it all. The advert breaks seemed endless, with each 30-second slot costing more than $5 million. When I see an advert starring Bill Murray for a new Jeep in the style of the *Groundhog Day* film I decide that it's time to retreat back to my very own burrow. I need to shower, sleep and get over a bit of jet lag.

New York City is arguably home to one of the finest railway stations in the world. Grand Central Terminal has been open since 1914, but the site has been a station as far back as 1871. Most people call it Grand Central Station, but it was originally known as Grand Central Depot. Once the main station for all the long-distance rail services leaving the city, since 1991 its forty-four platforms have just served passengers travelling on the Metro North Railroad system of New York State and Connecticut. Rather sadly nearly all of the grand trains now depart from Penn Station, a carbuncle beneath Madison Square Gardens, now in the process of being rebuilt. I want to pay a visit to this shrine of railroad history before leaving the city, even though my train won't be departing from this station. Walking up 42nd Street, the stonework of its façade sets the tone of its historical function as a gateway to the rest of America. Columns reach up from the street to a triumphal arch with sculptures and an ornate clock. I read that the granite blocks they are made from produces more radiation than a worker typically receives at a nuclear power station, so I decide not to dwell too long. But this actually has more to do with the stench of street life and stale urine around the outside of the building.

As I push through the doors, the real character of the station only appears as I walk down the passageway and enter the main concourse. It takes me a minute to let the sight sink in. Above on the vaulted ceiling is a vast mural of the constellations, for some reason painted backwards. Beneath this, in the middle of the concourse, is the information booth with a brass four-sided clock mounted on top. It was once valued at more than $10 million, when the faces were believed to be made of opal, which they are not. There is nothing obviously modern on display here, and you could easily imagine the same scene in front of you a century ago, but maybe with better hats. I could be here waiting to catch the 20th Century Limited to Chicago, just like Cary Grant does in the 1959 Hitchcock thriller, *North by Northwest*. The only thing I can see as a sign of current times is a huge American flag hanging against one of the walls, placed here in 2001 soon after 9/11.

Beneath the flag are a couple of police officers carefully watching people going about their business, and I assume also making sure that no one steals the clock. I've noticed all over the world that tourists from other countries seem happy to talk to police but locals avoid them at all costs. These officers are state police troopers and wear tailored grey uniforms and distinctive hats that remind me of the Gurkhas. One of them carries an M16 rifle, and the other seems to have a selection of handguns, batons and cuffs on his overloaded waist belt. I strike up a conversation about how smart they look and the need to stay in shape to look good in an outfit like that. But no matter what I do I can't get them to smile. My usual trick is to ask if they are not allowed to smile, but even that doesn't work. But it gets even worse than that: I notice the trooper with all the sidearms moving his right hand loosely onto the grip of his taser, presumably in case I turn out to be a madman. Obviously not a lethal madman, though, otherwise he would have gripped his Glock 21. I decide not to persevere with anything humorous in case it ends badly for me, and instead ask for directions to the Oyster Bar.

At the bottom of the steps to the track level is a low-ceilinged whispering gallery and at its end is the entrance into one of the great railway station restaurants in the world. Serving a wide range of seafood to hungry passengers since 1913, it opens its doors at 11.15 each morning, and in stream customers after something a bit more special than just a coffee and bagel from the surrounding sandwich chain stores. Inside, the terracotta tiled walls are covered in an eclectic selection of

interesting-looking junk, but before I can examine it all
I'm greeted by the maître d' dressed in a starched white
apron. He shows me to the bar around the corner in the
fashion of a much-missed regular customer. By my
calculation I was last here in 1989, so his interpretation
is rather generous. Over time many stations have
removed all their original dining facilities. I'm so pleased
this place has survived, as to me it is still the beating heart
of the station. Some customers even look in through a
take-away hatch and grab some chowder on the way to
their train. Can you imagine that on the 18.06 service
from Kings Cross to Hull?

The bar is still mostly empty and I choose a swivelling
seat near to an older man dressed in a tweed suit. I can
see he's a local, as the bartender knows what he likes to
eat and drink. I on the other hand have spent ten minutes
studying the extensive menu before choosing the New
England clam chowder, some local Beavertail oysters
and a glass of Colney Island Mermaid Pilsner. Beer
somehow tastes better when it's a local brew. Better still
if it's served by someone wearing a white apron. I have
no idea why. The bartender takes my order approvingly
and shouts it over to the chefs working with old-
fashioned appliances just behind the bar, who welcome
me over to inspect the day's catch. I suspect that these
people have spent their life working here and love what
they do. Big lesson number one, if New York has a
reputation for being unfriendly, I realise that this is
unfounded here. Loud, brash and no-nonsense maybe,

but very friendly once you get tuned into the humour.

It's just me and the man in the tweed suit at this bar today, and he's engrossed in his crossword puzzle, so I consult my notebook ahead of an afternoon's movie location hunting. You can't go far in New York without coming across locations where well-known films were shot. I love that sense of place – the very spot where the real-world transitions into the Hollywood fantasy. Sometimes completely false and with no synergy with the surroundings, but other times a genuine place with real locals as extras. From my swivel stool at the bar I realise that I'm already sitting in a recent train film location. I'm sat near to the table where Emily Blunt has a drink with her friend in the 2016 thriller *The Girl on the Train*. Tate Taylor's choice of commute is perfect. The book that the film was based on was set in a fictitious suburb of London, and it just can't compete with the amazing scenery on the Hudson line. They could of course have used the champagne bar upstairs at St Pancras, but the Thameslink commute would not have been nearly as visually impactful. Dreary home counties dormitory towns and scrapyards would never have worked as well as the lovely wooden houses upstate in New York.

My first objective in the afternoon is to find the location of the San Monique consulate. I have no plans to visit San Monique – it doesn't even exist. It's the tiny Caribbean island ruled by Dr Kananga in *Live and Let Die*. The film was released in 1973 and was the first to star

Roger Moore, a very different Bond from his predecessor. Whilst I liked Sean Connery, I was a child of the 1970s and so Roger Moore was somehow 'my' James Bond, and I envied his taste in fine cigars, roll neck sweaters and well-tailored safari suits. Having no luck in midtown, I moved on to 33 East 56th Street, the location of the Oh Cult Voodoo Shop. I recognise the building; it's not a voodoo shop any longer, but a luxury jewellery dealer. Bond tails a woman from here up to the Fillet of Soul bar in Harlem. That's the place where he gets spun around in a booth and captured by the evil Mr Big aka Dr Kananga wearing a mask. The Fillet of Soul was actually filmed on Second Avenue at 94th Street rather than Harlem, and sadly the ghetto constructed for the film bears no resemblance to its surroundings today. My first movie hunt isn't going so well today. More recently there has been a trend for directors to use real locations to add maximum authenticity to their films where possible. But filming a blaxploitation-style film in real-life 1970s Harlem was never going to be a winning idea. Never mind, I think. I will have to wait until I reach Louisiana to get back on the trail of Dr Kananga. His rather scary henchman, Tee Hee, even ends up fighting with Bond on board a Santa Fe sleeper carriage that would have been operated by the newly formed Amtrak. Roger Moore was definitely the most train-friendly Bond. He also fought off Jaws in *The Spy Who Loved Me* and the knife-throwing assassins on the rails in *Octopussy*.

When I'm not sat at the bar in Molly's, I'm a couple of

blocks away in my local diner, learning about local eclectic eating habits. New York is one of the most multicultural places on Earth, and whilst the place is Italian, its customers are Greek, Armenian, Sudanese and Korean. Breakfast here is the weirdest meal of the day. Fried chicken with waffles is quite popular, along with crispy bacon with a huge stack of pancakes. Or if you are in for brunch, perhaps a pastrami sandwich big enough to feed the whole neighbourhood. The only big mistake I make is with the bacon, which it seems might have originated from the wood-preparation aisle of a local DIY store. Bacon here, by law, must come from pork belly rather than the loin or shoulder. If you ever find yourself with this transatlantic problem, the solution is to ask for Canadian bacon, which approximates back bacon rather than streaky. The Canadians don't actually eat Canadian bacon, but it's what they supplied to Great Britain during pork shortages in the mid-1800s. Although I don't know it at the time, my breakfasts are to get weirder and weirder as the trip progresses.

I spend my final day in the Big Apple wandering round Central Park. I always end up walking too far when I'm in New York. I imagine Manhattan as a small place, but I still have to walk a few dozen blocks before accepting its true scale at over 30 square miles. I have memories of ice skating in the park one December and sunbathing on the grass in July, but today isn't a day for either, full of the fog and chill of winter but without the excitement of snow. You might not remember it, but this was also the location of a train action movie. In 1995 John McTiernan returned to direct the third in the Die Hard series, *Die Hard with a Vengeance*. There is some great chemistry between Samuel Jackson and Bruce Willis in this film, and the scene where Willis commandeers a taxi and cuts through Central Park to reach Wall Street station before a bomb goes off on the Brooklyn-bound 3 Train is really nicely done. 'I know what I'm doing,' says Willis to Jackson as they narrowly avoid collision with several vehicles whilst speeding downtown. A petrified Jackson yells back, 'Not even God knows what you're doing!' and 'Are you aiming for these people?' It's very much the last great Die Hard film. Keeping an eye out for any out-of-control taxis I wander up West Drive and past the Tavern on the Green and the Sheep Meadow towards The Lake.

Many people can remember what they were doing on Monday 8th December 1980. I didn't hear about the murder of John Lennon until the next morning. I had a broom in one hand and was trying to retune a very old valve radio to Radio One on the AM band in our dormitory at school. I occasionally visit Strawberry Fields when I'm in town, just for an hour or so. The feeling of the sense of place drew me once again across the street to The Dakota, once home to the Lennon family. Mark Chapman was actually a big Beatles fan, and asked Lennon to sign his copy of *Double Fantasy* only a matter of hours before shooting him four times on the steps outside with a .38 Special revolver. John Lennon was pronounced dead on arrival at Roosevelt Hospital at 11.15pm. Chapman became eligible for parole from his 20 years to life sentence at an upstate New York prison in 2000, but has so far been denied parole on eleven occasions. Strawberry Fields was dedicated in John's memory in 1985.

I hop on the 3 Train at 72nd Street and head down to Wall Street in a far more relaxed way than Bruce Willis managed. There isn't much to see here that appears in the *Die Hard* film, but it does of course also remind me of Oliver Stone's 1987 film of the same name. Like *Die Hard*, it is fully embedded into New York, from the stock exchange scenes down here on Wall Street to The Tavern on the Green back in Central Park where Bud Fox hands over his tape of Gordon Gecko to the FBI.

I find an amazing little Indian restaurant close to my hotel, where chef and I work quickly to calibrate his notion of how much chilli to use with my desire for something I would describe as 'spicy'. I deserve everything that I asked for. With the hiccups and the heat in my digestive tract still gradually subsiding, I perch on the bed in my room and watch a movie on my fruit-based tablet. There is a chair in the room, but it's not possible to get it out from the desk without having to balance it on the bed.

In 1987 Robert De Niro was such a big name that he could pretty much do whatever he wanted. Rather surprisingly, he wanted to stretch himself in a different way, and he chose a comedy for his next film. Turning down *Big*, which went to Tom Hanks, he chose *Midnight Run*, and the rest is history. The film was directed by Martin Brest, who had made *Beverley Hills Cop* and had a reputation for being able to blend action with comedy.

The plot of *Midnight Run* is a simple one. De Niro plays a bounty hunter, Jack Walsh, who has to get Jonathan 'The Duke' Mardukas, played by Charles Grodin, to a bail bond office in Los Angeles in just five days. Chased by Chicago mob boss Jimmy Serano and the FBI, he takes on a 'midnight run'. Of course, nothing goes to plan. The Duke pretends to have a fear of flying, so they have to get off a plane at JFK and find other means to get to LA. Their next form of transportation is by train, the Lake Shore Limited, headed to Chicago.

Midnight Run wasn't a massive box office success, but it is one of those films that has become better thought of over time, achieving almost cultlike status today. The critics say what makes it a stand-out film is the chemistry between De Niro and Grodin. But what I think makes it a seriously underrated film is that Yaphet Kotto, who plays Special Agent Alonzo Mosely, and Dennis Farina, who plays Jimmy Serano, are also at the very top of their game. Interesting to think that Paramount suggested Robin Williams play The Duke, and also Cher – but thank goodness Martin Brest stuck to his instinct that Grodin was the right choice for the part. There is a line in the script that absolutely nails the film to my first train journey – 'the Lake Shore Limited thunders past, into the night'.

Silver Streak

Chapter Three
Midnight Run

One of the most disappointing things about leaving New York by train is having to use Pennsylvania (or Penn) Station rather than Grand Central. Penn Station was once a grand building like its sister across town, but was knocked down to make way for Madison Square Gardens in 1963. Today its twenty-one tracks are all underground. In many ways, Penn resembles Euston station in London – it's a concrete bunker and a bit of a tip. But it's a busy tip, currently the most used passenger transportation facility in the whole of North America. The only silver lining of this dark cloud is that a brand new station is being built over the road at the site of the former James A. Farley Post Office. By the time you read this, it will be open.

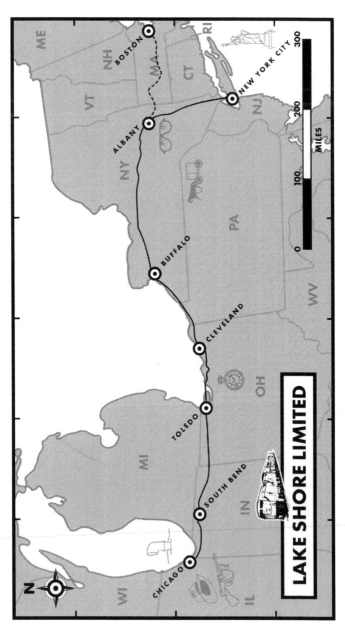

LAKE SHORE LIMITED

Hopping out of a cab and wheeling my bag along the sidewalk, I'm prepared for chaos inside, but things don't seem quite as bad as I imagined. The layout is confusing, as there are three different rail operators, each with their own concourse and their own style of signage. It's so confusing even for locals that a mobile app has been created just to find your way around the place. But by good fortune, after just a couple of minutes attempting to work out where I am, I accidentally stumble upon the Amtrak bag check-in desk. Unused to checking bags in for trains, I wait patiently behind a line painted on the floor between me and the desk. A couple of staff members behind the metal counter eventually notice me. 'What are you waiting for? Come on over, honey,' one says to me. The process is remarkably simple. A printed copy of my e-ticket has a bar code, which is all you need as far as tickets go. Once your bag is weighed and tagged, you get a little ticket to reclaim it at your destination. With everything done in a minute, I'm pointed in the direction of the Acela Lounge and wished a nice journey. So far so good.

The lounge is full of businesspeople waiting for the next express train to Washington DC. Mobile phones, laptops, and piles of cables festoon the small tables. I can feel their stress from the other end of the room. The joys of life on the rails as a pressurised executive. Big screens around the lounge show the status of arrivals and departures at the station. I had forgotten that you can take a train from here to Miami on the once futuristic

Silver Meteor – launched in 1939 as 'the train of tomorrow'.

My train today is the Lake Shore Limited, and I wait to be called from the comfort of a crazy reclining swivel chair which I feel must surely have been invented by a hip European designer with a pipe and cravat in the mid-1970s. Control of the chair is all about balance and gravity, and loss of control is assured if you relax too much in any particular position for more than a few seconds. From my jaunty position I can see the departures screen as well as the staff on the reception desk, who spend much of their time fending off passengers who don't have the right paperwork to use the lounge. But sleeper passengers always do, along with business class passengers on daytime routes like the one from here to Washington.

About 45 minutes before the scheduled departure time, the front desk announces that the Lake Shore is ready to board. To reach the train I'm given the option of a buggy with a Red Cap or an escorted walk. Red Caps are the Amtrak porters – smartly turned out and nearly always very friendly – probably because you're going to give them a large tip, but that's very much the way in these parts. I decide that the walk will be good for me, and make my way to the front of the lounge to meet my escort. It might sound like overkill, but I'm not sure if some of my fellow passengers now gathered around have been on a train before, and the layout of the platforms here is at first a bit confusing. It feels like a school outing. All that's missing are Paddington-style brown paper labels round our necks with our names on: 'From darkest NYC to Chicago. Thank you for looking after this bear'. I have absolutely no idea why finding our train isn't just about a platform number, but a bearing is also needed here in Penn. We need a westbound platform, so I hope our guide has set his compass to 270 degrees and taken into account any magnetic effects of the stone used to build the station. But he seems to know where he's going, and we follow behind in a straggled-out line. Should we hold hands in case someone gets lost? We eventually arrive at Platform 8 westbound, where the Lake Shore awaits us.

The Lake Shore Limited has been covering the 959 miles of track between New York and Chicago since the mid-1970s, but the two cities have been connected by trains under different names since 1897 when the Water Level Route was established by the New York Central Railroad. Today the Lake Shore also connects with a Boston service, the two Chicago-bound trains meeting up at Albany in the early evening.

Amtrak carriages are pretty distinctive, especially if you're used to European trains. Not many other railway carriages in the world have that bare metal fluted look. It looks both retro and futuristic at the same time, and very much in the spirit of Dan Dare. The Lake Shore's carriages are known as Viewliners, built in the mid-1990s.

If there were such a thing as an I-Spy guide to the American railroad, one of the first things you would learn is that there are basically two types of passenger carriages on the Amtrak network throughout America – Superliners and Viewliners. Superliner carriages are the double-decker ones. If you are American that's a bilevel car, or if you are European then it's a duplex. The Viewliners on the other hand are single-deck carriages. The reason for this is that Superliners can't safely fit through the tunnels at Penn and a few other spots east of Chicago.

Up front ahead of the set of Viewliners is a pair of shiny blue and grey P32DC-DM locomotives, known as the Genesis. The General Electric Genesis is the backbone of the current Amtrak long-distance fleet; most are the P42DC diesel version, but some, like this one, run on both diesel and electric power, as diesel operation is not permitted inside Penn Station. They are not high-speed trains: the theoretical maximum speed is 110 mph, but the maximum line speed for most routes limits the maximum speed to just 80 mph. The only real high-speed train currently in the United States is the Acela, which runs from Boston to Washington DC via New York City. But whilst it is capable of speeds over 150 mph, it averages just over 80 mph including stops, perhaps the reason it was rebranded from its original name, the Acela Express. Much of the Amtrak fleet is due to be replaced in the next few years, but as there is no point putting fast trains on a slow track, the new Siemens Chargers will still only be capable of 125 mph.

Outside carriage 4912 on the platform stands a man so tall that it looks like he will have to bend over in order to fit back into the train. I feel quietly confident that he plays basketball rather well. 'Big Robert' greets me with a smile and introduces himself, checking me off his paper copy of the passenger manifest. Welcoming me aboard he helps get my bag up the step and points me in the direction of my room. (Of course he doesn't call himself Big Robert – that's just how I will always remember him.) Viewliners have doors at one end of the carriage, a different layout from that of the Superliners, which have a central vestibule in the middle of the coach. Turning right inside, I pass the three ensuite bedrooms along one side of the carriage before twisting round to where the corridor runs between six compartments on each side. Except that this is America, and as we are not on board a submarine these are called roomettes. Each has two berths, one above the other – the lower one making up two comfy seats during the day.

I find my new home, roomette number 2, opposite Robert's crew room. Inside it's a small space, but I'm immediately happy to be here as it's comfortable and clean, albeit rather tired-looking. There is a flat space to one side of the pair of seats which I use to put all my essentials onto: camera, book, notebook, water bottle and an old Ghan amenity kit, now containing things like my lucky Swiss Army knife (which I'd bought in Hong

Kong to replace the less lucky one confiscated on my journey to Tibet), eyeshade and earplugs. The seats are wide and comfy, and a little table pulls out between them below a pair of panoramic windows, one above the other. I imagine that the top one is so that passengers sleeping in the upper berth can see out at night. I spot the charging point, the switches for the lights, and the controls for the air conditioning on a panel next to one of the seats. On the other side are some more controls with lights with coloured lenses that look like they might have been developed for the Mercury space program. The red one says 'sink down', the amber one 'toilet out of service'. That's handy, I think – a warning before setting off down the corridor to the bathroom. But there is a black button under this light that says 'toilet flush'. Surely the need for remote toilet flushing is a questionable piece of carriage design. How would you know when it's needed? Then it dawns on me. Underneath this little flat space is a toilet bowl, right next to the seat, and even closer to my head when it's converted into a bed. I'm not sure how to feel about this discovery, so I try to forget about it and pretend that it's not there.

Robert pokes his head in and he asks if I need anything. He's got other passengers to see, but he finds time to answer some critical questions about the plumbing and catering on board before excusing himself and heading down the corridor. It turns out that Viewliners have no toilets at the end of the carriage, just this commode in each of the roomettes. The dining car has no toilet either, but there are toilets in the regular coach carriages further down the train. It's no drama for me, but I wonder what research the designers did on the use of such a facility in a shared roomette, especially if the passenger in the upper berth needs to use the toilet when there is a person occupying the lower bunk.

In non-bathroom-related news, this train is running with a cut-back meal service known as 'flexible dining'. Amtrak has recently decided to simplify its food offering on its services east of the Mississippi, and this is one of them. Despite the marketeers pretending that this change is all about customer needs, the reality is that someone in an office far away from real passengers has decided to save money and run the catering in the style of a budget airline. I long for the Silver Streak dining experience, and take comfort that I have many freshly cooked meals to look forward to on other trains as I head further west.

With a couple of judders the train pulls out of Penn right on time. At first it's the darkness of the Manhattan tunnel network, until we eventually emerge into the open air and the grey daylight of the late winter afternoon. True to its name, as the Lake Shore heads north towards Albany, the tracks skirt the banks of the Hudson River and we quickly make the transition from city to the countryside. The concrete jungle shrinks behind us and gives way to wooden houses, fishing clubs, boatyards and a vista of forest on the far shore. I couldn't be more content, in my own space inside my roomette, with scenery like this. My first lesson is to not feel guilty about doing nothing other than staring out the window. I only wish it was a bit cleaner so I could take photographs that didn't have a strange filter of window grime. Taking a picture out of a train window is more of an art form that you might give it credit for. You have to decide if you are going to take the shot so that just the landscape is visible, or if the context of the train and its windows are going to be part of the composition. Then there are your worst enemies, the curves of the glass, the reflections of the lights inside the carriage, and the light-absorbing crust of dirt on the outside of the glass. Every shot is an experiment in managing these conditions. I decide to try the wide shot with the whole window and its onboard surroundings as the frame in my shot. But the windows are so large I have to step back into the roomette across the corridor to achieve this. Each time I turn the camera off and sit down, an even better view arrives, so I'm constantly up and down.

As the new boy on a new train I'm restless, so decide to explore. Grabbing my briefcase, I close the curtain that provides privacy from the corridor window, and slide my door shut behind me. You can't lock the door from the outside, but my feeling is this is a safe enough place. I head forwards, through to the dining car. I knew what to expect, but want to confirm it for myself. Where there would have been a busy carriage of interesting passengers, happy attendants and busy chefs, there's only one man in here, and he doesn't seem that pleased to see me.

Kurt is a tired-looking little man in his early 50s. At first I feel a bit sorry for him. His new role in the flexible catering system of this dining car is bartender, attendant, chef and the accountant of the cut-back service. His cooking duties, however, are limited to operating the microwave oven. Approaching the bar and counter area in front of me I smile at him, my best 'please be nice to me' smile. But he doesn't see this, as he is too wrapped up in the paperwork. 'What time do you want dinner this evening?' he asks. 'We got 6, 6.45, or 7.30.' Given I am yet to see a single other passenger and my meal is going to come out of a microwave, I wonder why a reservation is going to be needed, but I go along with it and tell him I'll see him at 7.30. I leave him to it and hope some atmosphere will arrive before my allotted dinner time. With nowhere else to explore I head back to my roomette to contemplate this arrangement. From the back of my mind I remember that Kurt was the name of the drunk chef in 'Gourmet Night', one of my favourite episodes of *Fawlty Towers*. I only hope that this is not a warning from television history of what might lie ahead.

The train passed through places with strange sounding names like Poughkeepsie and Rhinecliff before arriving into Albany at half past six. This is the state capital, a city that traces its roots back to Dutch and British colonists. Here, fur trading, railways and beer have given way to government and high-tech industry. Halfway from New York City to Montreal, this is the place we pick up the Boston carriages that are already waiting for us. The engineer doesn't explain the process, but we spend 40 minutes here organising passengers, bags, fuel and carriages before setting off and turning west toward the Great Lakes. If you are still thinking of the engineer as someone roving the train with a bag of spanners, then you're mistaken. It's the driver; it's all part of the dialect of the American railroad.

I return to the dining car clutching my dinner reservation coupon at the allotted time, where I find myself in a small queue at the bar where Kurt is taking orders. Making people arrive at a fixed time and queue might be efficient for him, but it makes the place feel like a cheap canteen. Even airlines serve meals at your seat.

'What's good?' I ask him when I eventually reach the front of the queue. 'We've got everything that's on the menu,' he replies, pushing a copy in my direction.

Flexible Dining Menu – Entrees

Red Wine Braised Beef
With pearl onions, carrots and mushrooms served with Polenta and Haricots Verts. Served with a side salad and a specialty dessert.

Asian Noodle Bowl
Yaki Soba noodles with carrot, edamame, red peppers, baby corn, scallions and Shiitake mushrooms in a garlic-chilli sauce. Served with a side salad and a specialty dessert.

Chicken Fettuccine
Roasted chicken with broccoli, carrots, red pepper, Parmesan and Asiago cheeses, in a garlic–alfredo crème sauce. Served with a side salad and a specialty dessert.

Creole Shrimp & Andouille
Shrimp & Andouille sausage served with yellow rice, peppers, onions and green onions in a Creole sauce. Served with a side salad and a specialty dessert.

Pasta & Meatballs – Kid's Meal
Penne pasta with tomato sauce, meatballs, Parmesan and mozzarella cheeses.

It reads well, and I opt for the chicken fettuccine. 'Knives and forks over there,' he points, pointing in the direction of the cutlery, salad dressings and sauces. The way it works here is that sleeper passengers have their meals included, but on a Viewliner the passengers in coach class are not even allowed in to buy meals. There is no table service for ordering, just the delivery of food on plastic trays. This differs from Superliners, where coach passengers are very welcome to come in for meals and pay for what they eat, which seems a little more civilised. 'You get one free drink,' Kurt tells me matter of factly. I ask for a white wine, a tiny bottle of Chardonnay, the only one on the menu. 'Is that your free drink?' he checks with me. This seems a bit odd, as though he thinks that I might pay for a drink now and consider having a free one later. Even though he's at the bar, he isn't going to let me have my free drink just yet, instead gesturing me in the direction of one of the unlaid tables at the other end of the carriage. This is beginning to feel a bit like a lunch at a primary school.

There are a few more people here than I realised were on the train. Most night trains run sets of two sleepers, with a dining car, a café car, and then two or more coach carriages, so these passengers must be from the other sleeper. Two couples seated opposite me appear to have already been tamed by Kurt and they are doing as instructed whilst remaining in good spirits. Amazingly the carriage has good wi-fi, and they are streaming local sports matches and chatting about the scores. One of the brilliant things about dining with Amtrak is the tradition it has of sitting people together. It's called Community Seating, and it's normally compulsory at all meals. But not on this train. With few passengers, and no laid tables or busy service I sit by myself. I don't want to sit alone, but no one else is sat at the single table with a cardboard sign proclaiming 'Community seating here'. With no waiters, no tablecloths, and no hubbub of passengers mixing, the place is soulless.

Kurt finally appears with my little bottle of wine and a microwaved meal for one complete with a side salad, all in little plastic-wrapped boxes. I toy with it for a while, trying to make the experience a bit more exiting but in a little over ten minutes I'm finished and bored. I order another glass of wine, which Kurt brings over and plonks on the table, and says 'There you go, Mr Moneybags.' He really isn't happy in his work, and to say he has a bit of a chip on his shoulder is an understatement. Alone and without the support and banter of working in a team he has gone a little bit mad, the soldier alone on the desert island 20 years after the war has ended. Thankfully this will be my only Viewliner on this adventure. It's okay here, but I'm pleased to get it out the way. It wouldn't be a good journey to finish my trip on.

Arriving back at my roomette I'm presented with a new challenge. Whilst I have been chewing my fettuccine Robert has pulled the seats down, added a mattress and made what looks like a comfy bed. The snag is that now there is barely 12 inches of floor between the bed and the door. With the door closed I can stand up but not really do anything easily, including changing into my complimentary pyjamas from a well-known airline. Eventually I figure it out and settle in, trying not to think about the commode next to my head. Tucked up in my bed with the lights dimmed I listen to the unfamiliar sounds of this new railroad at night: the 'clickety clack' of wheels crossing points and the 'clang clanging' of railway crossings mixed with occasional muted night-time announcements from the conductor. From time to time I glance at my wristwatch, which glows comfortingly in the dark and hopefully marks our progress on time towards Chicago.

On the night of 19th April 1891, train no 14, the Toledo Express of the Lake Shore and Michigan Southern Railway, was headed eastbound in these parts, on the two-way single-track line about 40 miles outside of Cleveland. Timothy Daly, the conductor, had the instruction to pull into a siding to let the westbound no 21 fast mail train pass by. Daly decided not to bother checking his own watch to see when he had to be off the main line, but instead let the engineer Edward 'Bacon' Brown, keep track of the time. Brown did so using his own pocket watch. Unfortunately, he did not realise that it had stopped working and was restarted by the motion of pulling it out of his pocket. He believed he had seven minutes before the designated meeting point of the two trains at Kipton. He left Oberlin, the station before, at 04.43 and knew they needed 6 minutes to reach the crossover switch in the track at Kipton, where they would then have a further minute to get off the main line and onto the spur track. But they actually had only 3 minutes and should have remained at Oberlin.

Charles Topliff, the engineer of the mail train number 21, was under instructions to maintain their full speed of around 40 miles per hour. He had his hand on the throttle and was pressing onward to reach Kipton on time. Barnes, the conductor, was keeping an eye on this too, but knew that his watch was running slightly fast and that he had to make allowances of around a minute. As they approached the tiny station the view ahead down the curved track was obscured by the wagons of freight trains on side lines. The Toledo Express crew saw the oncoming mail train and tried to brake, but it was too late – the trains collided and the mail train flew up into the air, landing on top of the Toledo Express. Amazingly none of the passengers were seriously injured, but eight railwaymen were killed, including both of the engineers. The heap of the wrecked trains was said to be taller than the station itself.

The enquiry by the inspectors and superintendents made several recommendations to prevent two trains ever meeting in this manner again, but the railway company, realising the equally important issue of timekeeping, employed Cleveland-based jeweller Webb C. Ball to develop a watch that would be more reliable for this purpose. Ball came up with a number of standards and produced a watch that would be reliable to within 30 seconds a week. These watches were to be the responsibility of the engineer and had to be regularly inspected to certify their timekeeping. It had to be able to withstand freezing winters, hot summers and the vibration and movement of the locomotive, and be visible day and night in the cab. This was to be the 'railroad standard'.

Observing the glow of my own watch, I feel a peculiar sense of its place and purpose. It's a Trainmaster Cannonball model, based on the original design of Webb

C. Ball's railway pocket watch. This will be my talisman for the trip, keeping me safe and on time. I hope that the engineer of tonight's Lake Shore has one too. But the words on the dial 'official standard' gets me thinking. How do you know if your watch keeps good time? Given what lies ahead, I decide to get it checked before the next leg of my journey, just as an engineer would have done with the dealers distributing the Ball watches in the 1890s. By 1910 there were more than 2000 jewellers inspecting over a million watches for 180 railroad companies. So, hopefully I can find someone in Chicago who will certify my Cannonball as fit for rail adventure.

Slowly I grow used to the rhythms of the rails and fall asleep. We pass through Buffalo, Cleveland and Toledo without incident and I wake up somewhere near the Ohio state border. Once I have managed to get dressed in bed, I pull back the curtains and slide open the door to my room. One of the things that I love about having a room on a train is that you can choose to keep the door open and chat to people or retreat into a private space with the door closed. No one is judging you. Outside the carriage is quiet, and I help myself to a cup of steaming coffee from the urn at the end of the carriage. Unlike the samovar that offers unlimited hot water on nearly every long-distance train in Asia, Americans like coffee, and sleeper carriages have a free supply of reasonably tasting filter coffee on the go most of the time. On this trip my portable espresso maker is redundant for the first time ever. Checking our timetable, we have a couple of hours to go before reaching Chicago, so there is time for breakfast, if I dare. I decide to go and see Kurt.

I find him just where I expect, fending off questions he doesn't want to answer from behind the bar top of the servery. He looks almost as unhappy to see passengers at breakfast as he did at dinner. This time I grab a menu without asking any difficult questions.

Continental Breakfast Selections

Oatmeal – *Maple Brown Sugar or Apple Walnut*
Cold Cereals – *Honey Nut Cheerios, Froot Loops, Rice Krispies, Raisin Bran*
Yogurt – *Strawberry or Blueberry*
Muffins – *Blueberry or Banana Nut*

Breakfast Bar

Breakfast Sandwich – *sausage, egg and cheese muffin*
Fruit – *Seasonal Fruit Cup or Bananas*

I choose the Breakfast Sandwich. Although it doesn't look very appetising from the picture on the menu, to my surprise it's actually pretty tasty. Although my doctor would not agree, there is something comforting about well-seasoned American sausage meat served in a bun. As I devour my nutritional time bomb I watch a Frenchman seated in the booth in front of me fall into Kurt's trap. He has ordered some Cheerios, and when he was asked if he wanted anything else with that he had said 'no'. His cereal arrived without milk, and he was nearly made to apologise to Kurt for changing his mind before he was allowed some.

Around 9 am we arrive at South Bend, the last stop before Chicago. Now a declining industrial town, South Bend was once the home of the Studebaker car factory until its demise in 1963. There isn't much to see from the train, and my only duty here is to adjust my watch back one hour to Central Time. At one time there were almost 100 time zones across the United States, causing all sorts of problems. The arrival of the telegraph lines helped solve them, and in the 1880s the country changed to just four time zones across its main land mass: Eastern, Central, Mountain and Pacific.

Big Robert checks in on me before we pull into Union Station to make sure I'm ready to go. It's just as well, as I have a paranoia about leaving things behind and scour every square inch of the roomette. Everything seems to be in order, but I repeat the process just to be sure. Once I'm down on the platform I thank him for looking after me. He says he hopes to see me again. I would be delighted to see him too – but I hope I never come across Kurt again.

Leaving the platform at Union Station is just a matter of walking down to the end of the tracks, where you enter the lower concourse of the station. I pause here, as this is an important location in the final scene of *Silver Streak*, but more of this later. Much, much, later.

The airport-style baggage carousel eventually starts beeping and when the belt starts moving I have my bag in moments. I hand the luggage master my ticket and once he is satisfied that I am the owner of my bag he points me towards the escalator up to the main hall. That's a great job title isn't it? Like being a dive master or a dungeon master, but with luggage. With hindsight, I should have found an elevator, but I manage to balance my bags on the wobbly stairs and emerge into the Great Hall without incident. The functional concrete construction below is replaced with marble up here, and I immediately feel a sense of the importance of the railroad to the city. The Chicago Union Station first opened its doors on 16th May 1925, and the floor tiles still gleam like new, illuminated from light streaming through the glass roof above. Polished brass lamps and Corinthian columns complete the Beaux-Arts look that must allow it admittance to the exclusive club of Great Railway Stations of the World.

Glancing up the grand staircase to my left, I see a smartly dressed man wearing a Stetson hat looking down on me as he helps a woman with an old-fashioned pram. My gaze then turns to passengers waiting on the wooden benches on the ground floor of the main hall. They seem unusually patient and peaceful for a railway station, as though the atmosphere created by the architecture has a calming influence on them. When I look back at the steps just a few seconds later the woman with the pram has vanished. How strange. That feeling of the sense of a place. Then the reason for its familiarity dawns on me. I am standing in the middle of the set-piece shootout scene in Brian De Palma's 1987 gangster thriller *The Untouchables*. Sean Connery won both an Oscar and a BAFTA for best supporting actor in the film, although I thought that his accent was a bit Scottish for an Irish-American – but not nearly as bad as his Scottish Russian accent in *The Hunt for Red October*. I mostly remember this film for the heavy use of Armani tailoring at a time of mass consumption of designer labels. I bought a double-breasted Armani overcoat on the strength of it, but it didn't make me look anything like Robert De Niro.

Chapter Four
Matthew Woodward's Day Off

Pushing my way through the big swing doors, I emerge onto West Jackson Boulevard and suck in the freezing air. It's a sunny winter morning and the glass-fronted buildings across the street are gleaming. But it's too cold to linger out here in my train-travelling attire, so I search for the warmth of a taxi, which takes about 10 seconds. Looking upwards from the back seat I can admire the skyscrapers as we follow the river northwards. When we pass by the shiny green curved glass front of 333 Wacker Drive I can't help but think that it looks very familiar. This is of course Ferris Bueller's dad's office from the cult 1986 classic movie *Ferris Bueller's Day Off.* The building was finished just before the movie was made, and it's now a much-loved part of Chicago's postmodern architecture. The film was a bit too cool for me at the time, possibly because although I was the same age as Ferris I could never imagine having a girlfriend like Mia

Sara, who played Sloane Patterson. But I'll never forget the scene from the film with the red Ferrari 250 GT California Spyder driving down Lakeshore Drive. Director John Hughes clearly loved his home town, and many of his films have been located all over the city.

The budget hotel off Michigan Avenue that I'm going to stay in hasn't got any rooms ready, so I have to resort to opening and repacking my bags on the floor in reception. This never looks very dignified, but I need warmer clothes and see no point in carrying my train kit around for the day. I guess that the concierge probably sees people doing this every day, and he gives me a little tag before wheeling my bags away towards the front entrance. I hope he is the concierge – what if he were just a random person dressed like a concierge with a pocket full of fake luggage tags? I can't put my finger on quite why, but at first my heart tells me that I like New York better. Hopefully some time here will challenge my preconceptions.

Like New York, Chicago is a city that is full of memorable film locations and it's not long before I accidentally stumble across one. As I walk down North Wells Street in the general direction of the city's Loop, the skyscrapers of West Wacker Drive once again tower overhead, but crossing the river from this direction I realise that I'm now right there with Harrison Ford in *The Fugitive*. This is the spot where Richard Kimble calls his lawyer from a payphone – one which doesn't actually exist in the real world. The US marshals hear the sound of the L (elevated train) and the bell on the Wells Bridge in the background of the tapped phone conversation. Whilst much of the film lives and breathes Chicago, the big train crash sequence towards the start of the film was actually shot in Dillsboro, North Carolina. A real train was used on a section of the Great Smoky Mountains Railroad, and everything had to be filmed in a single and expensive take of a real and full-on train crash.

The distinctive noise and sight of the L trains running above street level makes me think about one film in particular. Just a year after making *Ferris Bueller's Day Off*, John Hughes directed *Planes, Trains and Automobiles*. Some of the locations used in the film were actually a long way away from Chicago, but the scene towards the end, where John Candy and Steve Martin part ways, was shot a few blocks down the road from here at the La Salle–Van Buren stop, one of the busiest in the city. It's a scene of real compassion, one that always leaves me with a lump in my throat. I've never been a fan of Steve Martin, but this is a comedy double act made of pure gold. And anyone who has seen the film will be unable to ever forget the 'between two pillows, those aren't pillows' scene in the crummy motel bedroom. The story goes that John Hughes started out as an advertising copywriter and became stranded one day, travelling home from a client meeting in New York. This of course is used as the central plot of the film. Perhaps if he had taken the Lake Shore Limited rather than a plane, the movie would never have been made. I'm hoping to pass by some of the locations of this film later on my journey, but for now, though, I just have the film's zany soundtrack stuck in my brain as I head for a jewellery store in Wabash Avenue.

By the time I eventually reach the Diamond District my legs are chilled to the bone. It's almost Siberian out here – something to do with winds, Lake Michigan and the polar vortex. The chance to take refuge in a warm shop now has life-saving appeal, and I enter a big jewellery store to see if I can get my watch checked out. Upstairs is a room with miles of glass cases full of watches. There aren't many customers here today, and the staff are predatory, lingering until the moment when I look at a particular watch display for slightly too long. When I explain why I'm here to the hungry salesman he looks a little disappointed and decides he has no option but to summon a man called Jim. Jim is also a bit surprised by my request, so I explain the story of the Kipton crash and the role of the Ball pocket watch to him in a bit more detail. He finally accepts the reason why I'm here might be credible and decides to summon Michael. I sense that this sort of escalation is unusual in the store and wait patiently at the counter with the circling salesmen now eyeing me up from a more respectable distance. Now that Michael is involved I seem to have a bit more protection from them. He introduces himself as the manager of the store, and takes some time to inspect my Trainmaster in case, I can only assume, it might be a fake.

Removing his loupe he nods approvingly before taking my watch away to the back office for closer inspection. Once Jim realises that I'm definitely not in the market for a new watch he offers me a coffee and we talk about the city and its connection with the railroad. I'm enjoying our chat but it isn't long before Mike returns. 'It's a straight line,' he tells me in a reassuring manner, rather like a surgeon emerging from an operating theatre. I don't actually know what a straight line is, so he explains that this means that over a measured period of time the Cannonball was neither fast or slow – it is as accurate as it can be. Polishing it with a cloth, he returns it to me and wishes me well for my journey. It feels really good to have this connection with the railroad and its past. This is the watch equivalent of a religious blessing. With the comforting weight now back on my wrist, I'm down the stairs and back out onto the street.

You don't have to walk far in Chicago to come across signs of its prohibition past, and I had read about some of its more famous gangsters, like John Dillinger and Al Capone, on the flight to New York. I had no idea that Chicago had been through a period known as the 'beer wars'. At first this sounded to me like it might be an advertising battle between the big beer brands, but turned out to be about the criminal gang division between the north and the south sides of the city. There have been times when I have been in need of a glass of beer in a dry country, but I could not imagine going to war over it. But here in Chicago crime tripled during prohibition, and the black market for alcohol flourished. Some of the tell-tale speakeasy signs still remain across town to this day – green doors, car parks underneath buildings, and even tunnels under the streets. Chicago still remains the single most gang-infested city in the whole of the United States, although the murder rate has been falling since the 1970s. Yet in 2010 there were still more shootings here than in New York and Los Angeles combined. The part of town I'm staying in feels safe, but a couple of miles away the murder rate is ten times higher. Thankfully really good beer is now also freely available across the city.

My local speakeasy is a bar called Jack Melnick's Corner Tap. It's a great place to relax in. A stranger like me can pull up a stool at the bar, order a glass of tasty craft beer and join in the chat with the locals. The only downside is that it's normally about the incomprehensible sports shown on the huge televisions above the bar. But Jack Melnick's isn't just well known just for being a cosy sports bar. It's famous for its wings, and I don't mean the band The Beatles could have been. Plates of chicken covered in a range of unnaturally hot and sticky sauces are served to happy customers every day. Everyone seems to eat wings in Chicago; it's the go-to dish, perhaps more important than even a curry would be in my home town. The common bond in this place, though, is in the spice, the hotter the better. Next to the bar is a 'wall of flame', and if you're mad enough to finish a plate of the scorpion chilli wings then you're immortalised with a photograph. I like a hot curry, but looking at the expressions of the people pictured on the wall, I decide to go for just the hot wings rather than the killer scorpion variety.

I pair my wings with what has quickly became my favourite local beer, an IPA from the Goose Island Brewery. America has reinvented beer, with huge numbers of craft breweries springing up and offering tasty local brews. I often get into trouble when I tell my friends how good American beer is these days. Cask ale drinkers seem to view them satanically, but the point is they taste great and they have brought people back to enjoying good beer. The only irony is that the smaller brands are now being bought up by the bigger ones, and now even Goose Island is owned by one of the brewing giants.

There are a couple of other things that I'm keen to see before leaving the Windy City. You might not think that Chicago is a likely place to find one of the best-preserved U-boats in the world, but inside a specially built hangar in the Museum of Science and Technology sits U-505. At nearly 80 metres long and 10 metres high, the boat is enormous, far bigger than I had imagined. It ended up here in Chicago as this was the home of Captain Gallery, the commander of the American ship that managed to salvage and tow U-505 on 4th June 1944, despite attempts by the German crew to scuttle her. After a lengthy and top secret stay in Bermuda disguised as an

American submarine, USS Nemo, she was eventually towed through the Great Lakes in 1954. With support by many manufacturers of the original parts, the U-boat has been brought back to something close to her original condition.

A very well-trained guide called Janice met me at a visitor-sized hatch cut in the forward section of the port side of the U-boat. As she talked me through each of the compartments I became an extra in *Das Boot*, one of my favourite war movies, and had to stop myself practising dashing from one end of the boat to the other to help add forward weight in a dive. The detail of the restoration is incredible and I'm sure Janice regrets asking me if I have any questions at the end of the tour. Twenty minutes later she politely leaves me underneath the bow with some notes to read up on snorkel drills, films about U-boats and torpedo range setting.

I love all the submarine films that I can think of apart from one. I can handle Sean Connery and his lousy Russian accent in *The Hunt for Red October*. I can take the ludicrous school bully character of Gene Hackman in *Crimson Tide*. I can even stomach Harrison Ford in *K-19: The Widowmaker*. But what I just can't cope with is Matthew McConaughey in *U-571*. It's a film that perverts the cause of history to an extent that many found offensive when it was released in 2000. I mention this as the plot of the film was based on the capture of this very submarine and its Enigma machine. Examining the exhibits here today, I still feel the museum is slightly leading visitors towards concluding that it was the capture of U-505 in 1944 that cracked the code that had actually been deciphered at Bletchley Park in 1941. The film's screenwriter, David Ayer, has since admitted that the script distorted history and was something he would never do again. Even Bill Clinton called the film 'a work of fiction'.

I had quite a lot to think about on my cab journey back up the lake shore. My father sailed in a convoy from Greenock on the Clyde on board RMS Aquitania in 1945. He was on his way to train as a pilot in Canada with the Fleet Air Arm. He wrote in his diary on 11th April that docking in Halifax, Nova Scotia, had been delayed by an 'incident' with a U-boat, but commented no further on what sort of incident it was other than how good it was to get back on *terra firma*. Was this an example of the stereotypical British stiff upper lip, understating surviving a U-boat attack? I shall never know, but I can't help but think of the alternative outcomes of history. After the war Churchill wrote about how frightened he had been of the threat from the German wolfpacks in the North Atlantic. Were it not for the work in Poland and then at Bletchley Park in cracking the Enigma code I might not be here. Maybe that's why I dislike *U-571* so much.

Before heading south on my next train I meet up with James Devlin, an old work colleague from the drinks business who wants to give me a better grounding on beer and bars in the city. We sit at the long dark bar at the Clark Street Alehouse and sample a number of really good local beers. James moved here several years ago from his home in Glasgow, and I can tell he's very proud of both cities. I challenge him about the climate, the crime, and the terrible idea of deep pan pizza. He smiles sympathetically and encourages me to dive deeper on my next visit. Not just for the beer, but for the amazing summers on the lake shore, the blues, jazz and comedy clubs, and the architecture in different parts of the city. For the history of suburbs that grew from migrants, and how their identity still lives on today. I agree to come back again soon and wish him well before staggering back to my hotel, fortunately only a few blocks away.

According to the new dining laws of Amtrak, my next journey is going to be technically east of the Mississippi again, so I have to prepare myself for microwave-based catering in the dining car once more. I decide to supplement the Amtrak flexible dining menu with a picnic from my local grocery store. I have always found foreign supermarkets quite exotic. The challenge of finding something edible and the discovery of new and weird things that don't exist in your own supermarket back home. In the wine aisle I manage to find what looks to be an interesting bottle of Riesling from Washington State called Kung Fu Girl. Then there is the snack aisle full of bags of weird crisp brands. I have no idea what the difference is between a packet of Fritos and a packet of Cheetos, so I take both and a backup bag of nachos for good measure in case neither turns out to be edible. And from the fridge, a tub of Budweiser beer cheese. Only in America!

Silver Streak

Chapter Five
Southern Comfort

The City of New Orleans has connected Chicago with New Orleans since 1947, but a train known as the Panama Limited ran on this route from as early as 1911. Now a daily overnight service, it's a 934-mile journey that connects the two cities in around 19 hours, assuming everything goes to plan.

Inside the cavernous Great Hall of Union Station, I follow a sign saying simply 'To the trains'. That's nice and simple, and no surprise given that this is one of the largest railway stations in North America. Chicago is the hub of Amtrak, and most of its long-distance routes connect here. Although it is busy, the scale and design of the halls makes it feel peaceful even though this is the start of the early evening rush hour. Passengers wait on wooden benches that look like they have come from a church. What happened at New York's Penn station

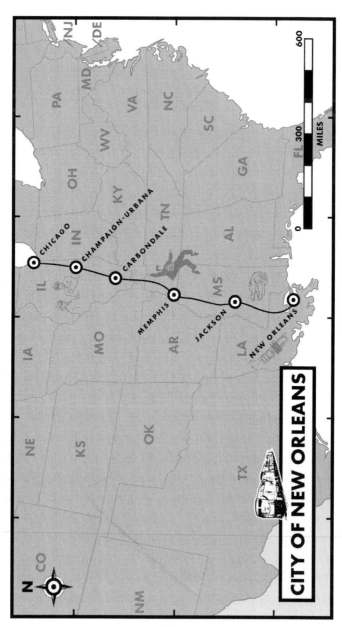

CITY OF NEW ORLEANS

hasn't been allowed to happen here.

My check-in this afternoon is smooth, and I have growing confidence in the system as I hand my bag over in exchange for a tag that has my destination initials printed on it. The phrase 'checked in' doesn't sound quite right for a train, but I shall use the term until I can think of a better one. With my bag handed over, the formalities are complete. There are no queues, no security checks. Instead I just wander around the corner to the imposing entrance to Metropolitan Lounge. Recently rebuilt in what was known as the 'headhouse', it is the largest of its kind in the United States, open only to business and first-class ticket holders – and that includes any passengers booked into sleeper accommodation.

I manage to find a comfy-looking chair in a quiet corner and put my things down so I can take a quick look around. Not only does it turn out to have the cleanest toilets and showers that I have ever seen in a railway station, it has a bar of sorts, and I treat myself to a cold beer. As the daily long-distance trains ahead of mine depart, the number of people left in the lounge dwindles until there are just a handful of us watching *Wheel of Fortune* on the big television screen. It's very different from the version that I have seen in the UK. The passengers seem happy to work as a team, calling out aloud to beat the contestants, so I stroll over to add my support until our train is called.

It's not long until an announcement confirms that our train is ready to board at platform 16. The layout here is much easier to follow than at New York Penn station, so I don't wait for the escort at reception but stroll at my own pace towards the gate, the door out onto the platform. I'm greeted here by the sight of double-decker trains on both sides. They tower above passengers and block out everything else around in the subterranean cavern. The carriages look deeply impressive. There are no narrow tunnels to worry about on this route, so the City of New Orleans is a Superliner. A pair of Genesis locomotives complete the train up front. They appear snail-like, hauling the much taller carriages behind, but this is the normal set up for Amtrak trains west of the Mississippi.

In the style of John Cleese in the much underrated film *Clockwise* (1986), I once almost left St Pancras station in London on the wrong Eurostar. As I was sitting in my allotted seat, it was only when someone with the same seat number arrived that I realised I was within a few moments of going to Disneyland by accident. Ever since then I have been really paranoid about getting on the wrong train when there are two sharing the same platform. This time, outside carriage 5900 of what I think is the right train I meet Lala. She finds me on her copy of the manifest, so I know I'm in the right place. I'm quite excited about being on a Superliner. It has the glamour that I associate with an aging jumbo jet: old, but classic, and of a scale that I'm not used to. My roomette is up top, so I climb the stairs and find roomette number 5 in the middle of the deck just past the coffee station. I immediately feel right at home in here. I twiddle a few knobs to check all is in order and decide it's a keeper. Unpacking is a personal ritual and takes just a minute, then I can sit back and relax. It's similar to a Viewliner, but not only do I have a more commanding view, but I'm also relieved to see there is no ensuite commode. Instead there are airline-style pressurised toilets, one on the upper deck and three more downstairs, where there is also a shower room.

Once we have set off, Lala makes a lengthy announcement on the PA about her expectations of her passengers for the journey. She runs a tight ship and explains in no uncertain terms that not flushing the toilet is a major offence, and if we don't keep her coffee station clean she will start charging for hot drinks. I'm not sure this is technically legal, but if it has the desired results then good for her. In fact, there are currently only three other passengers on the top deck of this carriage, so hopefully it will remain shipshape for the duration of our journey. But whilst I'm travelling the whole length of this route, the beauty of taking the train is of course that it can pick up passengers who might not have other transportation options. I would expect a steady stream of people getting on and off throughout the trip. I think that's going to be good for me too, as I'll get to meet more people.

Time to explore my new surroundings. The double deck runs most of the length of the train. Walking forwards from the rear of the train, I see two sleeper carriages followed by the dining car, and forward of this an observation car with the café beneath. The observation car is a great place for the regular passengers with seats in the two coach class carriages at the front of the train. Forward of them is what's known as a transition carriage, where the crew rest. It has an upper deck door at one end and lower deck door at the other in order to dock with the baggage car, and then a pair of locomotives. This is the normal layout of a long-distance train except on routes where the train divides to serve more than one destination.

Other than the transition car, the connection between the carriages is on the upper level. This means that other than the door to the platform on the lower level, in the sleeper the lower deck is just used for toilets, showers and a few different room types, including a family room that takes the whole width of the carriage at one end. You could argue for this reason that it's quieter below, but somehow being on the upper deck feels more premium. Underneath the upper deck of the dining car is a full kitchen, a place I have not yet seen. Under the observation lounge is the café, the place where coach class passengers get their meals, and where I can source cold beer. There is a huge amount of space compared to any other train I have ever been on. You don't feel confined to one place but can move freely between seats in several places.

It's not hard to find a seat in the dining car this evening. I haven't even been asked to make a reservation, which is the normal procedure. I find a seat at an empty table where I can look out in the direction we are travelling. Free seating might sound okay, but it doesn't encourage people to sit together. Downstairs, I imagine, are a range of shiny ovens, hobs and fresh food preparation services, all completely clean and idle, as this train runs on the flexible dining menu. Just one very busy microwave oven. It's not a massive menu, and here on my second journey I almost know its contents by heart. Deciding to opt for the creole shrimp with andouille sausage, I nurse a reasonably cold beer and make notes until it has been given some radar love.

Opposite me sit a pair of couples on a trip to Graceland for the weekend. In between checking the score in the Wildcats game, they divulge an Amtrak catering secret to me. The best thing on this microwave menu is the kid's meal option, pasta and meatballs. I make a note of this for my lunch tomorrow. My dinner sounds exotic, a taste of my destination, but if I were blindfolded I would only be able to distinguish it from the chicken fettuccine by its texture. I console myself that this is the last journey I'm taking with this new catering arrangement. What a disaster this is for passengers.

As I'm leaving, a couple arrive and I overhear them ask

the attendant what happened to the tablecloths, a question she ignores.

Lala tells me she's going off shift after the next stop, so I let her make up my bed even though I'm not planning on retiring just yet. We pull into a place called Champaign at 22.00, and it's snowing heavily outside. I hadn't really noticed the weather when we left Chicago, as the train was under cover at Union Station. Even though we are heading to the Deep South, for the time being we are still in Illinois and it's the middle of winter. Against my better judgement I decide to take a wander along the platform. Amtrak determines some stops as 'comfort breaks', which is code that you have time to have a cigarette on the platform. Lala pulls over the metal door handle that holds the door closed just by friction, pushes the door out and puts down a stepping stool on the platform. It's not exactly high tech. There are no automatic locks on the doors, no folding steps to lower down. Once I reach the ground I dip my boot into the powder on the platform to see if a quick snowman might be a possibility, but it isn't that sort of snow. There is no one else crazy enough to be out here to have a snowball fight with, so I hang out with Lala, making small talk. She's friendly, open and honest about things. Her walkie-talkie crackles with crew banter until the conductor tells the attendants, 'Three minutes, we're rolling,' which is my cue to get back on board so she can shut the doors and get some rest.

A visit to the bathroom before bed makes me feel like I'm on an airplane. Locked inside the little folding door, I find the environment cramped and vintage but perfectly functional. The only differences with an aircraft are that here there is no sign to tell you to go back to your seat, and that the little bottles of aftershave are missing.

This is my first night on the upper deck of a Superliner, and I'm surprised by the swaying motion, which seems much more pronounced up top. Maybe the track isn't very good on this route, as during the night I have vivid dreams about being at sea in a small boat. Woken by the motion at one point and lying awake in the darkness, I wonder what angle a double-deck carriage can roll to before it topples right over, but this is my mind playing tricks with me in the same way nervous fliers don't like seeing the wings bend in turbulence. Someone once told me that they won't snap even if they're bent vertically upwards. I hope Superliners can balance on very few wheels before gravity takes over.

When I draw open the curtains at around 6.30 the next morning we are pulling into Memphis. I had thought about stopping here for a couple of days, but I was keen to get further south as quickly as possible. With hindsight some local barbecue food and blues music would have been a great thing to do. Hurriedly getting dressed, I am just about to hop off when the conductor announces that we will be leaving soon, 'pulling on down to Greenwood,

Yazoo City and Jackson,' as we cross Mississippi on our way to Louisiana. Disappointed to not even get to share a platform with the King, I make my way back upstairs to get some breakfast where in the corridor I meet a man called Larry who looks lost. 'Where's the dining car?' he asks, and I tell him it's next door. He looks a bit unsure about this so I suggest that he follows me. I have noticed that some of the passengers on board need spoon-feeding every possible bit of detail. I think they must be older than I think they are but in very good shape so it's hard to tell, and no surprise they need a bit of help.

When Larry and I arrive in the dining car the attendant won't let us order breakfast until we decide what we want for lunch. 'Pasta and meatballs,' I tell her. 'That's a kid's meal' she says. I ask if that's okay, and with a sideways nod of the head she writes my order down and hands me a reservation slip. Maybe this marks me out as a seasoned veteran who knows his way round the flexible dining menu. I haven't seen any children on the train, but hope that they are free to choose from the adult menu. The carriage is pretty much deserted and I choose a table on the sunny side. Larry sits down at a table opposite me. He's either afraid of the sun or more likely of me. I decide to skip the cereal and muffins and order my breakfast sandwich.

The landscape has changed overnight. The tracks now pass through wide-open farmland plains with only the occasional sighting of a settlement. After breakfast I find my camera and head to the observation carriage where I find a spare row of comfy-looking seats. Everyone here seems to be happy and I'm not surprised. It's an amazing place to enjoy the views. The top deck is divided into two parts, half with bench-and-table seating just like the dining car, and the other half with rows of seats facing straight out of the windows along each side. In the middle is a small, so far unused, bar, and stairs leading down to the café below. The café has some seating on the lower level, but most passengers carry their purchases upstairs and enjoy the view from up top. The observation lounge and café are unreserved and free for anyone on the train to use at any time. I heard that Amtrak once tried to remove them from their trains as a cost-cutting measure, but the outcry from passengers was such that they were quickly reinstated.

At my seat I have a little side table to rest my coffee on, and in front of me a shelf below the panoramic window complete with charging sockets. It's the small points of attention to detail that make this carriage so good. But the best design feature of all is the quality of the light, with sunshine from windows overhead as well as the sides of the carriage. It's not long before I have fallen into a trance, staring out and occasionally sipping my Amtrak coffee, which I'm developing a taste for.

From time to time the train slows to a walking pace before coming to a halt in the middle of nowhere. It's a sensation that I'm learning to normalise. Amtrak actually owns very little of the track it runs on, and freight has priority over passenger trains. Where there is only a single track, passenger trains sit in sidings whilst freight trains pass by. They are incredibly long, and the carriages can take several minutes to rumble past.

But the reason for this particular delay turns out to be nothing to do with a freight train, but my first experience of refuelling. Seeing an oil tanker drive up next to the track and connect a hose up to the engine isn't something I've ever seen before. In the UK trains don't need to refuel, as they are either on comparatively short runs or powered by electricity, and in Europe and much of Asia it's more common to swap the whole engine for a fresh one. It takes half an hour to fill our locomotives up, and the engineer assures us this will be enough to pull us all the way down to New Orleans.

I like look at the timetable at the start of the day and work out which stops to get out at and which to ignore. The places that sound interesting, and stations where we spend more time at, are the ones where I try to get off. At some stops the conductor doesn't let you get off at all, whilst others are promoted as an official comfort stop. Today, there are only two or three of these.

As we cross the state line into Louisiana, it's not quite swamp land outside yet, but there are huge tracts of impenetrable muddy forest and occasional higgledy-piggledy villages. With some Ry Cooder playing on my headphones, I can only identify this as the landscape from *Southern Comfort*. I too am headed to Louisiana on weekend manoeuvres, but I hope to get on better with the Cajun people than the National Guard soldiers did in Walter Hill's memorable 1981 film.

The train slows as we pass a series of trackside wooden shacks, each with a shiny RV parked outside. This is a place where the size of your barbecue and your hot tub seem important. We pull up at a place that doesn't even seem to be on my timetable. It's called Ponchatoula. It's tiny and well maintained, and there are some neat horticultural features on the platform. There is even a small pond outside the stationmaster's office with something very unusual about it. It takes me a few moments to realise what I'm looking at. Two cold eyes staring impassively back at me. This station has a pet alligator. Before I can decide if it's friendly or not, Lala tells me, 'We're rolling.' Railway stations with pets or even zoos are an interesting subculture. I've heard of the importance of station cats in Japan and often seen bird cages on the platform in Thailand, but this is my first encounter with a station-based fierce creature. Can you imagine buying a ticket here for the first time? 'Carriage 1200, up the platform, near where the pond is, but don't hang around there as you might get eaten.' Lala tells me that Louisiana only has gators. Crocodiles live in Florida, and much further south. An adult gator can grow to 15 feet long and weigh 1000 lbs. It's the official state reptile. I don't think my home county of West Sussex has an official reptile, but I shall check on my return.

Talk of gators has me thinking about *Live and Let Die* again. It has always been one of my favourite James Bond films. What Roger Moore didn't have in suave sophistication he more than made up for in raised eyebrows and well-cut safari suits. Not forgetting of course, the blisteringly good Paul McCartney theme tune. The production crew went through no less than seventeen speed boats filming the iconic chase sequence around the nearby Irish Bayou, which is what most people probably remember it best for. The 100-foot boat jump set a Guinness world record when the film was made, but I think this part of the film is just too long – the chase lasted more than 12 minutes. As a small boy the scene that was most memorable to me is where James Bond escapes a grisly death by leaping across a series of crocodiles at a farm owned by Dr Kananga on his fictitious Caribbean island, San Monique. The scene was made by Ross Cananga, the real-life owner of the farm (actually in Jamaica), and he needed five or six takes to successfully jump across the backs of all the vicious beasts. On one take he didn't get it quite right, and needed 193 stitches.

We make good progress in the afternoon through the swamplands. The ubiquitous RVs are progressively replaced by small speedboats, which in turn are replaced by larger fishing boats as we emerge alongside waterways and lakes. In August 2005 New Orleans and its surrounding parishes were pretty much wiped out by Hurricane Katrina. Floods covered the city, and much of the transport infrastructure was destroyed: 200 mph winds and a 16-foot storm surge were more than the flood defences could handle. This was actually a moment for the railroad to shine, being for a time the only public transportation left working. The bridges we are crossing today have been largely rebuilt but the line connecting Louisiana to Alabama along the gulf coast still remains closed, fifteen years after the storm. There is hope that before too long it will be reopened, making a trip from Florida to LA possible once again.

You can see New Orleans from quite a long way away. Its tower blocks are in total contrast to the swamps. As we approach the outskirts of the city the conductor briefs us on a special manoeuvre that we'll need to complete before we arrive. It's a three-point turn, so that the train can back into the station and be ready, facing the right direction to leave. But the health and safety manual says that before such a turn-around, the engineer needs to test the brakes. Lala is on the PA several times asking everyone to sit down, as though she is calming an excited crowd boarding a rollercoaster. Eventually satisfied we are all clinging onto our seats, the engineer applies the brakes and we come to a gentle halt in a deserted railyard. So much for the violent deceleration.

Everything in order, we trundle backwards into New Orleans, a slightly dull and ordinary-looking station.

(Reflecting on that, I feel it's unfair, as almost any station would look a bit ordinary after Chicago Union.) I'm delighted to discover that Lala has been busy preparing a list of food and drink for me to try whilst I'm in her city. It's heavily weighted towards cocktails and fresh fish. I wish her well and say goodbye to the train before heading into the station building to wait for my bag. This has been a brilliant journey, only let down by the lack of real catering. But at least I know now that every other route I'm using from now on is running Superliners with full catering. I can't wait to travel on them – but first I have some plans for a long weekend in New Orleans.

To the amusement of my taxi driver I can't work out how to get into my hotel. I resort to trying a little dance outside as I assume that there might be a movement sensor. Eventually the concierge puts me out of my misery and presses a discreet button on the wall behind a bush. The heavy motorised doors slowly swing open, and I am met by a welcome rush of cold air. Reception is overflowing with people checking in for the weekend. A brigade of bellboys wheel trolleys loaded with serious amounts of luggage around the crowds of revellers and into the lifts. The atmosphere is party-like and the place smells of exotic booze, aftershave and good cigars. When I eventually reach the reception desk, I ask the woman behind it what's going on. 'This is New Orleans, sir; it's like this here every day.'

My room is enormous – not that I'll be spending much

time here, but it's nice to have space to get dressed without having to stand on the bed. I sense big rooms and casinos are part of the package to promote tourism in the city. Hotel rooms in New York City and Chicago are tiny unless you have a big budget, but here the norm seems to be more apartment-sized. I don't want to waste any time, so after sorting out my tickets and paperwork for the next leg, I unpack some clothes for the warm and humid climate. Inside my bag I discover a shocking packing fail. In Chicago I bought a big bag of chocolate ginger chews, and these have split and dispersed themselves amongst my clothes. Chocolate plus heat equals something that might resemble the dirty protest of a giant rabbit, so I have to forensically examine and repack each item before it's too late.

Walking up Canal Street it's immediately clear to me that this is a city like no other I have previously encountered in America. It's only late afternoon, but most of the people I pass are inebriated to the point of staggering. They carry cocktails and beers in plastic glasses or, as I find out, 'to-go cups'. The alcohol laws here are unusual to say the least. Firstly, in the French quarter you can drink in the streets as long as you have a suitable plastic container. Unlike in the rest of the United States, people aged 18 or over can drink alcohol if they are accompanied by someone over 21. Bars can stay open 24 hours a day, and they actually have drive-through stores selling frozen daiquiris. I spot a convenience store and pop in to see what's being sold – always a good sign of what's going on when in an unfamiliar place. The man behind the counter looks up and then ignores me, that thousand-yard stare of someone who has seen it all. The store seems to stock all the key items that might be needed here. An aisle full of party costumes, beads and silly hats, several aisles selling alcohol, and an aisle selling vaping and smoking equipment, including a massive humidor full of non-Cuban cigars. I pay for a bottle of mineral water and step back outside into the low sun on the big street. Most of the cars are hot rods and supercars driven by implausibly young-looking men. How do kids here have access to the heavy metal, I wonder? If this were Blackpool or Skegness they' d be lucky to get insurance for a Ford Focus.

Turning right into Bourbon Street I negotiate groups of dazed and confused drinkers deciding what to do with the rest of their evening. Some have clearly never heard the expression 'pace yourself'. Crowds spill out from bars unevenly from either side of the street, and the balconies above are jammed with people shouting down to people over the cacophony of the soundtracks. The police quietly observe from a discreet distance, not wanting to spoil anyone's fun. I had hoped that Bourbon Street was going to be a good place to soak up the atmosphere, but I now I'm here I feel that this is the last place on Earth that I want to spend the evening in. I skirt round a few blocks looking for a more suitable establishment, and eventually settle on a large bar with a sticky floor and bored-looking staff. The range of beers on offer is stunning, but they won't let me drink out of a proper glass in this part of town. Plan B is to leave the French quarter and find somewhere more grown-up to relax in – as the Spice Girls once famously said, to zig when the others zag. This works, and on the recommendation of the concierge I discover a well-run bar with good food hidden behind my hotel.

After the indulgence of a night in a proper bed, I'm late up on Sunday morning, and when I open the curtains the sun is high in the sky, the heat on the windows fighting with the room's air conditioning for climate supremacy. It looks like a wonderful day to explore the city. I find a seat at the bar in reception where I find that the coffee is free, but such is the atmosphere of the place I'm soon talked into a cocktail upgrade. The bartender says he makes the best Bloody Marys in the city and has his own secret recipe. I don't normally drink in the morning, but in this place with what I have planned for the day ahead, it might just be my salvation.

If you ever saw *Live and Let Die* you might remember the scene in New Orleans where a secret agent outside the Fillet of Soul club is watching a procession pass by and asks a man on the sidewalk 'Whose funeral is it?' 'Yours,' replies the man, and stabs the agent in the side before the brass band scoop him up in a coffin and continue their march down Chartres Street, switching their tempo from solemn funereal pace to a higher-energy dance. These processions still take place on most

Sundays in New Orleans. The ritual is said to have been brought to the city by enslaved West Africans especially for their funerals. Steeped in etiquette, the main parade is made up of the official band and the family, followed by a 'second line' of pretty much anyone else who wants to join in. Today that's even going to include me.

Time flies at the bar, and glancing at my Cannonball, I realise that I need to get going. I have to find the starting point of the parade before it leaves – a place which is on the edge of what the concierge tells me is a no-go area at night. The taxi driver knows the spot and takes me as close as he can. My invite says 'This is a family affair. Keep your troubles, attitude and weapons at home'. But I need not have worried, as when I find North Rampart Street everything seems just fine. However, this could be the result of the anaesthetic effect of a couple of seriously good Bloody Marys.

The side streets are cordoned off to traffic, and emerging onto the main road on foot, I join hundreds of fellow second steppers. Most people are waiting on the sidewalk in front of a throng of some cool-looking performers doing their warm-up routines. They are dressed in bright yellow designer suits with matching Louis Vuitton accessories. I have clearly misjudged the dress code, but I do have a brightly coloured handkerchief to wave and a willingness to learn. The band practise their routines, and mounted police look on through a curtain of smoke from the portable barbecues and dope. Everyone seems to be playing nicely.

No one seems too worried about time-keeping, but at around midday the leader of the parade waves his pace stick and kicks off the routine. To begin with I follow them alongside, but decide this isn't the time to be stand-offish, and join in behind the parade on the road. The crowd on in the second line is large and at times I become overwhelmed in a sea of celebrants throwing various shapes. I must have stood out just like Roger Moore at the Fillet of Soul, but without the sartorial elegance of his suit. Following behind the band, we make steady progress along the planned route, pausing for short stops at various funeral homes, barber's shops, clubs and hideaways. A parade of floats follow behind us, and finally the mounted police. As someone who genetically has no rhythm in their body, I just walk and wave, occasionally throwing the odd rave move with my arms. Small fish, big fish, big box, little box. This seems to satisfy those around me that I might be a true stepper. A man close to me has come better prepared than me. He steers a trolley with a large cold box on top, packed with icy beverages. He tells me that I look just like his cousin Stewy, and that he's going to look after me.

I have decided beforehand not to go all the way to the disbanding point, where a party is promised at a place called Kermit Ruffins' Mother in Law Lounge. I'm already deep in a part of town I'm not too sure about, and whilst the atmosphere in the group is good, I'm out of my depth here. In the thrill of the moment I almost change my mind, but then I spot a road name that I think I recognise, and decide to call it a day. I wave at everyone one final time and duck out under the rope that is being carried around us. Did I really just do that? I need a beer.

New Orleans has some lovely old streets with pretty Creole cottages and townhouses, and the walk back to the French quarter is really nice in the shade of the buildings. After getting lost a couple of times, I turn into Frenchman Street, famous for its buildings and its bars. It's quiet here at this time of the day, and there are no kids drinking on the streets. This is much more the city I'd been looking for yesterday. Sitting at the bar with a glass of NOLA Blonde beer, I listen to the live bands for a couple of hours before making my way home past the French market and along the river front.

The huge variety of food on offer confuses me for much of my stay. I have no idea what the difference is between cajun and creole cuisine, and I'm not sure if either or both are also called soul food. It all seems to be mixed together on the menus in the places I frequent on the edge of the French quarter. Eventually I pluck up the courage to admit my ignorance to a waiter who I judge might be sympathetic to my cause. He picks up a menu and suggests a few choices of the best from each. Creole is the food of the European colonial settlers in Louisiana. It's a fusion of all sorts of cooking. Cajun food is based on the cuisine of French-Canadian settlers, generally with less fish and more spice. Soul food turns out to be something different altogether, coming from the African-American descendants of slaves. I have heard of some the more famous dishes like jambalaya and gumbo, but still have no idea what a po'boy was, or why dirty rice is dirty.

As the weekend draws to a close I wander down a street I think I know, looking for somewhere to try out my new-found culinary knowledge. I look into the windows of several places, but most are either too formal, or too touristy, or are dive bars. When I find myself in this situation, I often turn to my Buddhist method of restaurant selection: just follow someone who looks interesting – you never know where it might lead. Looking up and down the road, I don't fancy following a lot of the people on the pavement. But eventually I see a chap carrying a violin, and tuck in behind him on the way down towards the river. He makes a couple of turns, and just when I have begun to think he might be heading home, he ducks into a little back doorway which has no signs on it. Following the building around the corner, there's a sign: 'Mulate's', it reads, 'the original Cajun restaurant. Nightly live Cujun band'. Okay it *is* a bit touristy, but the Buddhist navigation technique seems to have paid off once again, and I push through the doors. Inside there is a big dance floor, wooden beams, and lots of tables adorned with red checked cloths.

The specialty is catfish, cooked in several different ways. I choose a grilled fillet with a thing on top called a shrimp étouffée, a kind of stew, and jambalaya, the rice part of the dish. The chap I followed on the street joins a group of musicians on the stage and they start playing cajun blues music that I learn is called 'zydeco', a local style of rhythm and blues. I recognise it from the final scene of *Southern Comfort* where Keith Carradine and Powers Booth are taken to a pig roast at the Cajun village. Fortunately, my evening is more relaxed and involves no escape through a swamp.

Chapter Six
Local Hero

The following morning I'm up before most of the guests staying at my hotel have gone to bed. Down at the station everything is quiet and calm, the check-in the most airport-like experience yet of this journey. Large counters dominate the view at the front of a characterless but airy hall. The man who takes my bag points out a door in one corner of the station that I hadn't noticed. As I'm in a roomette, even for just the day today, I'm allowed to use the Magnolia Lounge. It's high security stuff. Armed with a little piece of paper with a code printed on one side, I make my way over to the locked door. Judging by the size of the room, there are few VIPs travelling by rail in these parts. There is hot coffee in one corner and a television showing the news, which always seems to be about escaped large and dangerous animals. Passengers in the lounge greet new arrivals like it is some sort of private members' club.

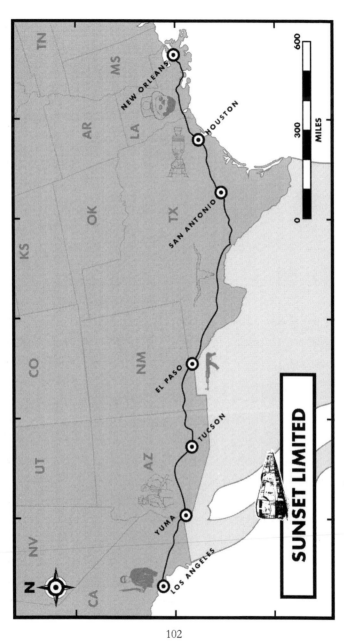

SUNSET LIMITED

NEW ORLEANS
HOUSTON
SAN ANTONIO
EL PASO
TUCSON
YUMA
LOS ANGELES

TN
MS
AR
LA
OK
TX
KS
NM
CO
AZ
UT
NV
CA

N

MILES
0 300 600

I've noticed that unlike in Britain, people in the US expect more than an answer of 'good, thanks' or 'okay' when asked how they are. They expect to be able to chat about your answer. This is rather refreshing to me, as I've always hated the falseness of the ultra-brief answer that hides a multitude of possibilities.

The well-prepared here have brought some breakfast with them, as there is nothing obvious for sale in the station. I pour myself a cup of coffee and rummage in my bag where I find a beignet, a little square pastry covered in powdered sugar. The combination gives me a bit of a kick and together with the sunlight I'm in a good mood and excited about the day ahead.

The railroad from New Orleans goes west all the way to Los Angeles, nearly 2000 miles away, but my plan is to travel to Houston next, where I will take a short break. The only complication with this plan is that the train that I'm using, the Sunset Limited, doesn't run every day, so I have had to work around its three-times-a-week timetable. Probably for this reason, it is the least used of all the Amtrak long-distance trains. My journey to Houston will take eight hours, just 300 miles away across the border into Texas. On reflection, I need not have booked a sleeper room for such a short trip, but when making the bookings I hadn't thought about this. Dr Kananga's one-armed henchman in *Live and Let Die* didn't even reserve a seat in coach on this train. The final shot of the movie is of him riding on the bumper of the locomotive, after being thrown out the bedroom window by James Bond.

The Sunset Limited used to connect Orlando, Florida, to Los Angeles, but since Hurricane Katrina the line east of New Orleans has been closed. It's actually the oldest named rail route in America, dating back to 1894 as the Sunset Express. Avoiding the brutal winter weather in the Rockies, it connected New Orleans to San Francisco in a little over 71 hours. Today it shares part of the route with another train called the Texas Eagle, which comes down from Chicago to San Antonio, Texas. From here it runs in conjunction with the Sunset Limited through to LA, making it the longest of the Amtrak routes if you combine the journeys of both trains.

Now used to the boarding drill, when the train is called I feel relaxed enough to hang back and chat with some of the other passengers to find out where they are going; some to El Paso, some with me to Houston, and just a few all the way to LA. It's quite different from getting on a plane, where there is often a bundle to get to your seat first. When most people have passed through the ticket check at the gate I go through and stroll down the platform. Train number 1 sits outside in the bright sunshine awaiting its passengers. At the door to carriage 0130 I meet Paul, my Texan attendant for today's trip. He crosses me off his list and shows me up the stairs where I'm in roomette 002, opposite the crew room. On first inspection the crew room looks very similar to any other roomette, but above the door, out of sight from the passageway, there is a control panel with various lights and signals showing which rooms have rung their call bell. I settle in opposite and wait for blast-off. Right on the ball at 09.00, the engineer gives a blast on the horn and we roll out of the station, picking up speed and heading west. Before long the city skyline falls into the distance and the tracks became progressively elevated from the flood plain made of 'gumbo soil', the silt from the Mississippi river. In front of us is the metalwork of the Huey P. Long Bridge, which the train will need to cross, over 150 feet above the river. One of the longest rail bridges in America, its truss of cantilevers makes it quite a sight. I often encounter a weird sense of fear of falling off big bridges, butterflies in my stomach and a need to hold onto something. Gripping the arms of my seat, I'm happier once we have made the crossing.

One of Amtrak's worst ever disasters occurred in 1993 when three locomotives and eight carriages plunged off the Big Bayou Canot Bridge in Alabama and exploded in the canal below. Very sadly, 47 people aboard the Sunset Limited were killed and a further 103 were injured. A towboat had become lost in the fog and struck a supporting span of the bridge. Fate had a hand in the accident, as the train had been delayed leaving New Orleans by half an hour to fix a faulty toilet. Had the train left on time it would have crossed the bridge before the boat hit it. I learn from one of the crew that a derogatory nickname for the Genesis locomotive came directly from the incident: some call them Mud Missiles.

'Are you having lunch today, Matthew?' Paul peers in from the corridor. 'I got 12.30 and 1.15 left.' A welcome distraction from thinking about rail disasters. I'm intrigued by the times on offer, and they herald something very different about this train; a working kitchen and a full menu. When I check, Paul proudly tells me, 'We gotta chef on board.' I choose the later time, and Paul hands me a slip of paper that confirms my reservation. I hold it firmly in my hand like a Willy Wonka golden ticket to lunch at the chocolate factory.

I have time for a wander, and as we are now safely back to ground level, I decide to walk through to the sightseeing lounge. In the corridor of the sleeper I can see that Paul is highly organised. At the coffee station, he doesn't just offer fresh caffeine but orange juice as well, and even a small library of paperback books. Nothing really to my taste, but still something to read if you ever become bored of chatting or staring out of the window. Basil Fawlty would describe these paperbacks as transatlantic trash, but I'm not being judgemental. I do, however, think that the episode of *Fawlty Towers* called 'Waldorf Salad' is a wonderful way of showing how different British and Americans are in the way we communicate. Mr Hamilton, the well-travelled American, is assertive, confident and straight to the point, compared to the English residents of the mad hotel, who are guarded, non-confrontational, and embarrassed when they don't get what they want. For several generations after the Second World War, causing a scene in public in Britain was seen as Bad Form.

In the observation lounge a dozen or so passengers bask in the sunshine, looking out over the river. I join them and settle down with a cup of coffee. What fool would pay for a roomette for the day when they could sit comfortably in this wonderful space? Only me.

I've been struggling to really get going today, and I realise it might have something to do with the sleeping pill I took last night. Americans have an interesting and often troubled relationship with pharmaceuticals. In most of Europe it's not possible to buy painkillers in packs of more than 16 or 32, but in the US you can by huge jars of hundreds of pills, and they are not kept behind the counter. The manufacturers even blend pain killers with sleeping pills, and the one I took from my large jar yesterday made me blotto in about five minutes. I read somewhere that by putting pills in plastic blister packs the suicide rate in Britain was nearly halved, something that doesn't seem to be a concern here.

Suburban life in Louisiana seems to involve a lot of toys. In the back gardens of most of the single-storey wooden houses are collections of trampolines, paddling pools, jet skis and boats on trailers. Out front, the obligatory flagpole and a shiny RV. Every third home also seems to have a weekend sports car. Something muscly and butch, usually a Ford Mustang, but occasionally a Chevrolet Camaro or Dodge Viper. The cars and boats are often in better condition than the homes they belong to.

Downstairs in the café bar Scott is busy selling snacks, mainly to the passengers in coach class. His words on the PA are full of wisdom: 'Sit back, relax, and enjoy your time on board.' But shortly we will pull into Lafayette, a 20-minute stop, and I decide that I'm going to stretch my legs. I head back to carriage 0130 and watch Paul get ready. He opens the window in the door and peers outside down the length of the train. It's not a small window, more of a barn door.

At the front by the locomotives, I meet Jeff, the conductor. He wears a uniform with a peaked cap and a waistcoat, and has a smartly trimmed beard. If it wasn't for his walkie-talkie, he might have dressed the same for this job in the 1930s. There isn't anything much to see here, but it's good to have something to do. If trains in Britain stopped for any length of time I would get off them as well, even though I might be a bit worried about losing my seat or my belongings – but I don't feel that's at all likely here. Jeff tells me he's having a busy day, and he's going to have to stop again up ahead to get off and manually switch the points. Thinking of the 2010 film *Unstoppable*, which you'll hear more of later in the book, I decide against telling him to make sure the throttle is set to idle before he does this.

My reservation time for lunch is called once we are back under way, and I share a table with a Mexican film producer, a Texan rafting guide and a truck driver. This never happens at a restaurant in the real world, where we nearly always eat with people we know, people we work with or people where there are more obvious things in common. Over lunch this time, we spend an hour chatting about various things, including gentle politics, news and current affairs.

The menu is a great improvement on the click-and-ping dishes of the last two trips, and it takes me a while to work through it:

Lunch

Romaine Entrée Salad

Romaine lettuce with dried cranberries, grapes, red onions, almonds, walnuts and pecans. With your choice of dressing and a warm roll.

Black Bean & Corn Veggie Burger

Spice, full flavoured veggie burger on a toasted bun with lettuce, tomato, red onions and kettle chips.

Natural Angus Burger

Grilled antibiotic and hormone free Angus beef burger on a brioche roll with lettuce, tomato, red onions and kettle chips.

Baked Chilaquiles

Layered corn tortillas with chicken, chorizo, egg and cheese, with chunky salsa, tomatillo-cilantro sauce and Parmesan cheese.

Steamed Mussels
Prince Edward Island mussels in a white wine and garlic broth.

Garden Salad
With choice of dressing.

Toppings
Cheddar or Monterey Jack cheese
Guacamole
Applewood smoked bacon

The children's menu also offers a Hebrew National All Beef Hotdog or Macaroni and Cheese.

I decide to join the rest of my table with the Angus burger. The attendant recommends a cheese and bacon upgrade, and I go along with his wisdom. Les, the film producer, makes outward bound films and has recently had an enquiry from a well-known television adventurer asking if there are any five-star hotels in his area. But most of my interest is in Bradley, the truck driver. He doesn't say much and sits upright to attention throughout lunch like he's at a work interview. It turns out he's headed to home to pick up a rig and a container of undisclosed highly explosive chemicals. Dressed in a grey sweatsuit, he looks a bit like he might have been recently released from detention but, given the nature of his work, I hope not. He tells me he's getting off at a place called Beaumont. I ask him what the place is famous for, but he doesn't think it's famous for anything.

When we arrive at Beaumont later in the afternoon I'm struck by the smell of the sea. Salt, mud and weed. It turns out that it's a port and home of the first-ever rice mill in Texas. Today, though, it's part of major industrial area on the Gulf Coast, and a more recently discovered oilfield, which I guess is why Bradley now lives and works here.

We pull into Houston slightly behind schedule in the early evening. Behind the platform the skyscrapers are lighting up, accompanied by a chorus of the many thousand birds who have made the station their home. A vintage agricultural tractor arrives to collect the baggage and bring it the 50 feet into the tiny station building. The lady behind the ticket desk lends me the office phone, and it takes me a few minutes to explain to the taxi company where the railroad station in Houston is. 'That's right,' I tell the operator, 'the Amtrak train station, 902 Washington Avenue.' She sounds doubtful but says she will send a car to that address. How can a taxi company not know where their railway station is? The size of the station also tells part of the story. One of the largest cities in the country has just a single platform and a building about the size of a small McDonalds. (See what I did there? Americans understand the size of a McDonalds.) The city has chosen to ignore the railroad in favour of the automobile and the rocket. Welcome to Space City!

I check into a business hotel in a cheap part of the city. Tired and a little unsure of the neighbourhood, I find the bar, seat myself on a high stool and order a local beer called Spindle Tap Hop Gusher. The bartender is a friendly Mexican called Marcos, and you can tell he knows most of his regulars well enough to be on first name terms with them and pour them their drink before they need to ask. I'm discovering that hotel bars serve a slightly different purpose in America, not just for one-night businesspeople or people engaged in meetings, but locals who like the slightly clubby atmosphere. 'Another beer, Mr Matthew?' Try the tacos – they're *excelente*!'

The man seated opposite me on the other side of the square bar asks Marcos if he can cash out. This is a phrase I hadn't heard before, but I realise it means to pay the bill, along with a nice tip for Marcos, who wishes him goodnight with the slightly chilling phrase 'drive carefully'. Tucked against a pillar on my side is a man I hadn't noticed before. He wears a big black cowboy hat, something I'd be quite scared to do in my local watering hole back home, but it's very normal here. At first, Travis ignores me in favour of a fresh copy of the sports section of the Chronicle, but Marcos introduces me and I gather as much intel as I can on what it's like in this part of town. What I mean of course is will I get mugged, but I don't ask him that. He tells me it's fine out there, but he carries a .357 Python to be extra safe. Better stopping power than a straight .44, he assures me, as though I might arm myself with one tomorrow. Finishing his cocktail, he excuses himself and leaves me to think about that fact over my meal.

The most remarkable thing about my otherwise drab and plain business hotel is the manager. He seems to always be on duty, well dressed in a slightly Texan way, with a well-pressed light-coloured suit that would be seen as too casual behind a reception desk in more formal cities. But what's remarkable about this man is not his dress sense but his power to know your name and what you are up to. Not just your name, but everyone's name. 'Gooood morning, Mr Woodward, how are you this morning? It's going to be a nice day. Enjoy your breakfast.' How does he do that? I think of him lying awake at night revising. Or does he have a hidden earpiece?

I have only been in the US for a couple of weeks, and already I have learned a few certainties about the great American breakfast. It always comes with breakfast potatoes, bacon that is hard and brittle, and eggs of your choosing. It's the law. But here in Texas there is a new protocol to observe. Texas toast. 'What's the difference between ordinary toast and Texas toast?' I ask the waiter. He thinks about this for a while, and I begin to expect a complex culinary explanation, but he eventually comes up with the answer that it's made with thicker slices of bread.

This hotel is great if you're keen on cars, as just off to

one side of it is the Gulf Freeway, winding round the edge of the inner city. I get a bit lost in identical-looking blocks of the downtown area. But I fondly remember a couple of the buildings from a scene filmed here in one of my favourite films. A character called Mac MacIntyre drove his white Porsche 911 turbo on this very road, with his office in the background which was set in both the Texas Commerce Tower and at Pennzoil Place. In 1981 David Putnam and Bill Forsyth were busy with the script of their forthcoming film *Local Hero*, which was released in 1983. It had a lot of cues from the television soap opera *Dallas*, and the city was chosen to be the home to the headquarters of Knox Oil & Gas, whose executive, Felix Happer, was played by Burt Lancaster. Made on a budget of just £3 million, it became a cult film, much loved by almost everyone who has seen it. Although mostly shot on location in Scotland, the Houston scenes revolve around Felix Happer in his huge glass office. The outside shots were of the Commerce Tower, and then some internal filming was done at Pennzoil Place – amazingly, in real life the actual office of one George H.W. Bush. But the final scenes were actually shot inside the Ben Nevis Distillery in Fort William, where the same office was recreated. Strolling up Smith Street and turning onto Travis Street in search of the right bus stop, I peer up at what is now called the JPMorgan Chase Tower, and think of Burt Lancaster staring up into the sky looking for the constellation Virgo.

My mission today is to visit the Johnston Space Center

on the outskirts of the city. (And see what I just did *there*? – I spelled 'centre' like an American.) It's my main reason for stopping in Houston. The American space program might have launched all its rockets from Cape Canaveral, but mission control and NASA's centre for human spaceflight have always been based here. More than 100 buildings were constructed in a 1600-acre campus, hence Houston being known as Space City.

The bus driver isn't hanging about today. I'm not sure if this is because her schedule is tight or if she just fancies getting off her shift early. As we pull across junctions around the freeways to the south-east of the city, I wonder if it might help keep all the wheels on the tarmac if I were to shift my weight from side to side. I've seen Jan de Bont's 1994 film *Speed*, but that was filmed on the highways of Los Angeles. Hopefully no big bus jumps will be needed today. A man called Tom gets on the bus at an out-of-town car park and takes the seat behind me. Wearing a baseball cap and smart checked shirt, he looks preppy and friendly enough, and we chat about things that keep my mind off our bus, which is now weaving in and out of slower traffic on the interstate. He tells me that he wants to travel to Thailand, not just soon, but tomorrow. His questions become increasingly weird, and it doesn't take me too long to realise that he's under the influence of something quite potent. At first he makes quite a lot of sense, but his grasp of reality seems to be going downhill fast. He decides to stand up, and props himself upright just behind the driver, who now seems even keener to reach the next stop. Bored of swearing at her and taking photos with his phone, he staggers back to pick up the conversation with me again. In between moments of crazy Tom, out come some interesting thoughts. 'Matt, why don't you start your next book at the end?' he suggests, before slipping into a deep session on values and beliefs. I'm uncomfortable ignoring him, but talking to him just sets him off on fresh rants. All I can do is to smile and nod a lot.

The driver finally pulls into a parking lot and he has to get off. I feel a bit sorry for poor Tom. I wonder what led him into getting into that state of addiction. A few years ago I watched a documentary about the Houston drugs scene, and it transpired that a lot of people had developed prescription drug addictions from work injuries, before switching to cheaper and easier-to-find street drugs, mainly heroin, fentanyl and methamphetamine. The problem is still on the rise, and apparently ambulances can hardly keep up with the demand to resuscitate people on the street. The driver of this bus has clearly seen it all before, and she apologises to me as she drops me outside the entrance to the Space Center. Starting my book at the end. I'll have to think some more about that.

You can't really miss the right stop to get off the bus. Independence Plaza towers above you, with a mock-up of the space shuttle Independence mounted on top of NASA 905, a converted 747 jumbo jet (which is still flight-certified to this day). The day flies by as I visit buildings around the campus with some very well-informed and educated guides. There is a real thrill in sitting in the modern-day Mission Control and watching relaxed-looking scientists and managers pointing to readouts on their monitors as the International Space Station passes by 253 miles above the building. My guide explains that this room will be used for the next moon landings in less than five years' time. She also points out that the first human to land on Mars is possibly in the room now. I always think of NASA in terms of its past achievements, but here, today, Hollywood science fiction is fast becoming science fact.

It's a grey day outside and light rain blows across the campus. The longhorn cattle grazing in fields between rows of buildings don't show much interest in either their surroundings or crewed spaceflight. I'm told to look out for deer and alligators, but they are sensibly hiding somewhere more comfortable on a day like today. Next stop is Building 30, the Christopher C. Kraft Mission Control, home to all the Apollo missions and a few of the shuttle ones too. A palpable sense of history and of place can be felt as I climb the flights of stairs that lead to the control room, or at least the VIP room that looks onto it. I find a seat towards the front. I'm told to look after it – it's still covered in the original orange cloth of the late 1960s. In this very seat, on this very fabric, astronaut wives and senators would have taken their places to watch the historic Apollo missions. More than

650 million people watched Neil Armstrong and Buzz Aldrin land on the moon on 20th July 1969, and part of the show on networks around the world were following every move of the ground controllers in this room. I've had this strange feeling of personal connection with a historic event in other places before but, other than perhaps the spot where Nelson fell on the deck of HMS Victory, none as powerfully as here and now.

The original dull green consoles in the control room are arranged around a huge overhead screen onto which all the mission data was projected. Old-fashioned valve monitors glow at the desks which have simple analogue features like rotational dials and illuminated buttons. The panels are riveted into position, but include handles so they can be removed for maintenance in the same way that the repairer might deal with a family television. A simulation of the moon landing is shown, and it literally is just like being there, albeit at another time. This room would also have heard Apollo 13's commander, Jim Lovell, announce those words, well known from the movie, 'Houston, we've got a problem'. Except of course he didn't say that. The actual words were first spoken by Command Module Pilot John Swigert, who said, 'Okay, Houston, we've had a problem here,' repeated by Lovell on request from the ground, who added, 'We've had a Main Bus B undervolt.' Hollywood rewriting history for cinematic effect. Flight Director Gene Kranz never said 'failure is not an option', either – but it sounded great in the script of Ron Howard's 1995 film.

Building 30 was officially abandoned in 1992, opened up just for occasional VIP tours. Visitors had been souvenir-hunting over the years, and gradually things had gone missing and the room had begun to look nothing like its former self. After much work, in 2019 a fully restored control room was opened by the great man Gene Kranz himself. Original fixtures and fittings had been recovered from all over the NASA complex, right down to period cigar boxes, coffee mugs and staplers. I wonder why Ron Howard chose to recreate his own mission control at Universal Studios in Hollywood rather than use the real thing. *Apollo 13* was a hugely successful film. It turned a budget of over $50 million into $355 million at the box office. I can't imagine anyone other than Tom Hanks playing the part of Jim Lovell, but rather scarily I have discovered that John Travolta turned down the role and that the studio had also originally planned for Kevin Costner to play the part. On this occasion I think Hollywood got the right man.

On the way back to the hotel I pop into a local wine store to pick up a bottle of something interesting for my next train journey. I remember a line in *Apollo 13* when Tom Hanks, as Jim, walks into a party at the Lovell household with what he calls the last case of champagne in Houston. However, had he chosen to visit this local wine store, he would have been reassured: past the private security guard with the shotgun, I find a warehouse with every conceivable type of wine, including mountains of champagne. The staff have all the time in the world to chat about wine and anything else on your mind. I'm deeply impressed with the depth of knowledge of the man who assists me, and using lateral tasting ideas, he finds me something interesting even in my budget.

When I tell him I'm off on the train to LA tomorrow he's quite surprised. 'How do you do that?' he asks. 'I've always wanted to take the train. My favourite film is called *Silver Streak*. Do you know it?' Half an hour later we swap scraps of paper. His contains a list of the best wines in California for under $20 a bottle. Mine contains the route of the Sunset Limited and the address of the railroad station in Houston.

Closer to my hotel I walk past a shop with a singular focus on selling hats. Hundreds of them, in every shape and size. Dare I wear a hat for the rest of my adventure? I would need to wear it not just here in Texas, where it's perfectly normal, but also in states where I might look a bit out of place, or worse still, like a tourist. I decide to consider this further and head inside. Perhaps I could pull off the look of Paul Newman in *Butch Cassidy and the Sundance Kid*? Rows and rows of hats in cupboards, and pictures of famous people on the walls wearing their hats. Amongst the selection I notice that they even have a railroad engineer's cap, but I fear it might make me look like a cross between Elmer Fudd and a recently released sex offender. Try to imagine yourself wearing it at home, I tell myself. I don't want to be like one of those people that you see at the airport returning from Mexico wearing a huge comedy sombrero, or from Vietnam with a conical straw farmer's hat. But these worries don't apply to locals; here in this city it's possible to wear an outrageously camp wide-brimmed white cowboy hat without anyone even giving you a second glance. In fact, it probably helps you to blend in.

High up on the wall I notice a hat that I think looks quite cool, and the man behind the counter spots me admiring it. 'Do you fancy trying a few on, sir? I'm sure I can find the perfect one for you,' he tells me, taking on the role of the fez-wearing shopkeeper in the fancy dress shop from my favourite children's cartoon programme of the 1970s, *Mr Benn*. This shopkeeper doesn't wear a fez, though, because this is Texas. Instead he sports a rather stylish black felt cowboy hat. If you have travelled with me on one of my adventures before, you will know about the significance of Mr Benn and the Mr Benn moment, when Mr Benn returns to his home at 52 Festival Road and discovers an object from his most recent adventure in his pocket to prove it really happened. This has happened to me a few times, pulling strange objects out of my jacket and remembering amazing people and places. But this is the first time I have ever actually been in the equivalent of the fancy dress shop. And here I have the opportunity to choose the outfit for my own adventure. It's not lost on me that David McKee, the series creator, actually wrote an episode titled 'Cowboy'. The plot is that Mr Benn helps some cowboys to win a game of hide and seek with the Indians. It sounds safe enough now, but I worry that over time the message of the plot might become overthought and misread.

The shopkeeper pulls some hats down, placing them on the counter, and in a well-practised manoeuvre takes my head measurements. He promises me he will find the perfect hat for the shape of my head, but I think this is coded language that I'm definitely not going to look like Butch Cassidy. I try a few on and stare at myself in the mirror, imagining what people would think of a man wearing a hat like that. My confidence growing, I decide to ask for the hat that I really want to try on. It's a very particular hat, made famous by a character in one of the greatest films of modern cinema. 'Do you have a Colonel Kilgore?' I ask him.

Apocalypse Now was eventually released in 1979 after a lengthy production delay. It was shot almost entirely on location in the Philippines, and the production team had needed to cope with a typhoon destroying the set, a civil war, disease, Michael Sheen (who plays the central character, Captain Willard), having a heart attack, and the drink and drugs problems of several actors, some having even stopped talking to each other. You could write a book about it. In fact, Francis Coppola's wife Eleanor did; it's called *Hearts of Darkness: A Filmmaker's Apocalypse.*

I hope you have seen the film in one of its several

versions. There are many stand-out characters and moments, and whatever your views are on whether it is really pro- or anti-war, it is a masterful spectacle. For me it's certainly the best film made about the American war in Vietnam. In case you haven't seen it, Colonel Kilgore, played by Robert Duvall, is surf-loving cavalry commander who helps escort Captain Willard upriver to find and terminate Colonel Kurtz, played by Marlon Brando, who has set up base deep in the Cambodian jungle. Duvall isn't actually in the film for very long, and I can recite all his lines pretty much perfectly. A formation of helicopters flies low across the river delta and attacks the village at Charlie's Point to the soundtrack of Wagner's 'Ride of the Valkyries'. On landing, Kilgore ignores the intense fighting and sets about some surfing with boards strapped to the sides of his Huey chopper. In the beach scene, the lines that so many people know by heart, from 'You smell that? Napalm, Son. Nothing in the world smalls like that. I love the smell of napalm in the morning' right through to 'You know, someday this war's going to end'.

Kilgore is based on a real-life officer, possibly several. He's as mad as a box of frogs, unconventional, and loved by his men. The 9th Cavalry play the bugle before take-off, and of course Kilgore wears his cavalry version of the Stetson hat except when he's in his helicopter. I guess it would blow off when the doors are open. There is actually a continuity error to look out for when you next watch the film. Before they take off he wears a hat with his rank and crossed sabres beneath. On landing his oak leaves have been replaced by just a larger pair of crossed sabres. If you watch the Redux version of the film the hat cords are also wrong for his rank; he's a colonel, not a warrant officer. But this is hat detail that I'm going to keep to myself today, I decide. I'm not even sure if the shopkeeper would know who Colonel Kilgore was, but I need not have worried. 'Oh, you'd like to try the Kilgore?' he says. approvingly. 'Coming right up!'

He positions the hat on my head and we both stare at my appearance in the large mirror behind the counter. Huey helicopters fly past in the background. Men with surf boards. Napalm. The smell of victory. But somehow the hat makes me look more like Colonel Saunders of Kentucky Fried Chicken fame than Colonel Kilgore. The proportions don't seem quite right. Robert Duvall just looks more butch and manly in his version. The shopkeeper knows that too and confirms it might be a little bit too big for me. Disappointedly I hand it back and thank him for not laughing at me.

I'm about to make my excuses and leave the store when I remember the Mr Benn moment. In the 'Cowboy' episode Mr Benn discovers a sheriff's badge in his pocket on the way back to his home in Festival Road. The shop has a whole display of these, and I find one that has 'Texas Ranger' engraved on its lone star. I pay for it and leave before I make any rash hat-buying decisions. I hope it will bring me good fortune.

Back at the hotel the manager is there waiting for me in the lobby. 'Good day, Mr Woodward. How were things out at Johnston today?' Most disarming. He presses the lift button to my floor without asking what floor I'm staying on. I bet he'd have saluted me if I'd been wearing that Colonel Kilgore hat.

It's time to pack and get ready for the next leg of my journey. It's my first two-night train trip, so I have a bag of provisions to squeeze into my day bag. Amtrak charges $8 (plus a tip, so $10) for a glass of wine, and although you can't drink your own booze in the lounge or any of the public areas, it's perfectly okay to bring your own bottle to consume responsibly in your roomette. I'm pleased with what I have picked up at the wine store. Amongst the small selection is a Pinot Noir from Oregon made by the Francis Ford Coppola winery. It seems rather appropriate.

Silver Streak

Chapter Seven
3.10 to Yuma

The following day I arrive back at the railroad station to catch the Sunset Limited, this time all the way to LA. It won't of course be the same train that I hopped off two days earlier, but another one on the same route. The ticket agent who helped me get a taxi a couple of days ago recognises me and makes polite small talk as she takes my bag away to the back room to be weighed. Amtrak don't accept bags over their 50lb limit, but you can check in more than one bag. I don't know why my bag is getting heavier, but it's still just under the weight. Satisfied all is in order, she gives me a tag and tells me to take a seat. I realise how incredibly relaxed I have become about taking trains in America. The only downside is if your train gets delayed. When the train has originated from a long way away there is more chance of the delay building as it gives way to freight trains, and stations like this one have few facilities to pass the time.

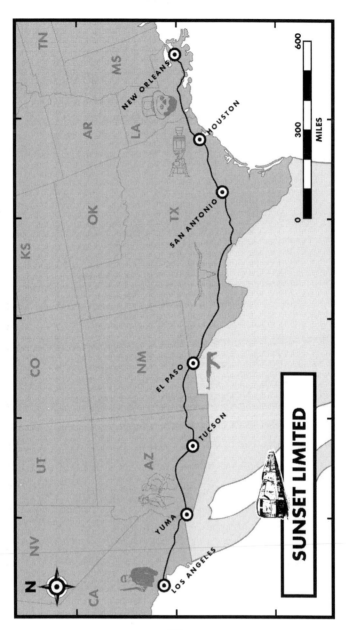

SUNSET LIMITED

N

NEW ORLEANS
HOUSTON
SAN ANTONIO
EL PASO
TUCSON
YUMA
LOS ANGELES

TN
MS
AR
LA
OK
TX
KS
CO
NM
UT
AZ
NV
CA

0   300   600
MILES

Train number 1 left New this morning and, eight hours into its journey, is now running just 30 minutes behind schedule, so I decide to watch *Wheel of Fortune* again with a few other passengers until it arrives. An elderly lady sitting right in front of the television screen tells me that she has been playing since it first went on air in 1975. It's becoming part of my standard pre-boarding routine. Playing alongside me is a friendly Mexican woman with several handbags. She's going to LA too, but in coach class. She is resigned to 36 hours in a seat, and I feel rather embarrassed to admit that I'm in a sleeper. We agree to try and meet later in the observation lounge.

Daylight is fading when the Sunset Limited pulls in. The lights on the first locomotive are bright, and behind them the platform lights reflect off the silver sides of the coaches. We form a short line by the door and are eventually released onto the platform by a member of staff. Passengers are not generally allowed to wait on platforms in the United States; it's more like the airport system of waiting at the gate until the train is ready to receive passengers. I'm back in the same carriage number this evening, but this time in roomette number 6, further down the corridor than on my last trip. Madeline introduces herself as the attendant and helps me settle in. The carriage looks a bit older and more lived-in than the previous one, and I can spot a few subtle differences that identify it as an older design. The most obvious is the lack of a little wardrobe to hang things in my roomette.

I'm looking forward to this next leg. It's a longer journey than I have taken so far, and there should be some real wild west scenery. Texas is a huge place. The train will still be in Texas at lunchtime tomorrow, when it reaches El Paso, where Texas, New Mexico and Mexico meet. The distance from here in Houston to LA is 1632 miles, and I'm going to be on board for two nights, giving me plenty of time to settle into the routine of stops, meals and time in the observation lounge.

In the dining car I find a jovial waiter called John wearing a beanie hat and thick-rimmed glasses. He smiles warmly and books me in for the next sitting. There's a real buzz in here and it's all down to the staff looking after their customers so well. I'm seated at the far end of the carriage with a couple of new age-style travellers on the way back to San Francisco and a chap called Grey who's headed back to his home in El Paso. John comes by to take our order. He's a real people-pleaser, and I immediately love his approach to everything. He takes an order for drinks and makes a note of our room numbers; if you give him a room or roomette number he knows not to bill you for your food, as it's included in the ticket. All that's left for me to do is make the difficult decision of what to order from the menu.

Dinner

Land & Sea Combo
Cooked to order, USDA Choice Black Angus flat iron steak

with a premium lump crab cake and optional Bearnaise sauce.
Served with vegetables and your choice of baked or mashed potato,
or a wild rice pilaf.

The Amtrak Signature Steak
Grilled to order, USDA Choice Black Angus flat iron steak
with optional Bearnaise sauce. Served with baked potato, sour
cream and baby green beans.

Norwegian Salmon
Seared Norwegian salmon fillet with sauce of the day, with rice
pilaf and baby green beans.

Thyme Roasted Chicken Breast
Thyme seasoned chicken breast with mashed potatoes and baby
green beans. Served with a complimentary sauce.

Rigatoni Pasta
Al dente rigatoni pasta with oven roasted tomatoes, mushrooms,
peas and vegan soy sausage.

Garden Salad
With choice of dressing.

Desserts
Vanilla pudding, Flourless Chocolate Tart, Up Town
Cheesecake, Seasonal Dessert.

I go for the thyme roasted chicken, Grey chooses a
well-cooked steak, and the girls go for the vegan option,
rigatoni pasta. 'Let me see if I've got this right,' John says
as he repeats the order. 'Very good – are you going
to try the cheesecake?' Nearly all John's sentences are
topped off with encouraging words like a 'very good!'

or 'I got ya!'

Once again, I realise that there are few other social contexts where the four of us would be eating a meal at the same table. Grey tells us about his daughter and granddaughter, who he's moved to be with in El Paso. Since his wife died it's all he lives for. He's living life in his own bubble and has little interest in anything else. The girls headed to San Francisco turn out not to be new age hipsters. They might dress that way, but they are actually both founders of separate start-up technology companies, one of which is huge. I've wrongly judged these books by their covers. I reposition them in my brain as the 'hippy CEO start-up kids'. For people so young, I guess in their mid-20s, they are incredibly sharp, and interested in learning about absolutely everything. I sip Chardonnay from my plastic glass and listen to them inventing things right in front of me.

Well after the cheesecake has arrived, the final stop of the night is San Antonio. There is some work for the crew here, as this is where the Sunset Limited combines with the Texas Eagle. On the platform, I meet a British woman who is a nurse in LA and we admire the Spanish-style station building with stucco walls and clay roofs. It's been here since 1877. Behind the cuteness of the station, the lights of the distinctive Tower of the Americas shimmer in the night sky. The station looks great at night, but there is an odd atmosphere. As I am wandering down towards the locomotive a man steps out of the shadows and asks me where I'm going. He wants to know what I'm doing here. Telling him that I'm both a rail enthusiast and a passenger doesn't seem to cut much ice, and as my eyes adjust I can see he's a private security guard – complete with bulletproof vest and large old-school handgun. In no uncertain terms he tells me to be careful and to stay with my own carriage, so I head back to find Madeline. There is something not quite right here. It looks nice, but in the middle of the night maybe this isn't the safest place in the world. I feel safer standing beside Madeline, but she's not saying much about the need for armed security here. I wonder if this is just a petty theft problem or at the other end of the spectrum, something to do with the cartels. I have clearly been watching too much *Breaking Bad*. When the sleepers and a second set of dining and sightseeing carriages from the Eagle are finally hooked up, the new-look train is twice the size of the one that left Houston. The engineer blows his horn, and we climb back aboard. This isn't the sort of place you would want to be left behind in.

Sleep comes quite easily and I enjoy the gentle motion of the train as we make progress westwards in the general direction of the Mexican border. I dream about a mixture of weird things. That's quite normal for me. I'm used to the dream where I lose my luggage and miss the train. I'm also used to the one where I'm back at university studying for a degree that I already have. Answers on a postcard, please. But in the waking hour after dawn, I dream of breakfast. A proper freshly cooked American breakfast on a train. My suspicions are aroused by the continuation of the dream after I have opened my eyes. A dream within a dream perhaps? I hear a quiet voice in my head. It says, 'Pancakes, coffee, omelets,' then a minute or so later, 'We got waffles!' This is in fact not a food-based dream, but Eggi in the dining car whispering on the PA to get passengers out of bed and into an early breakfast. I've never heard anyone else whisper on a train PA before. I would encourage it – it's certainly better than those British trains with someone shouting and repeating things every few minutes of the journey.

Behind the curtains, it's still Texas out there – now with strangely shaped limestone outcrops and desert plains. Consulting my watch, I work out that it's the middle of the afternoon back at home. I need to speak to Sheila from my PR firm about a Scotsman with a huge model railway in LA. I look hopefully at my phone, but unsurprisingly it has no signal. I'm in the middle of nowhere, or on the rails to nowhere.

All is quiet in the dining car and I settle down to breakfast. The other passengers haven't yet been seduced by Eggi's clarion call, so I study the menu alone:

Breakfast

Scrambled Eggs
Two fresh scrambled cage-free eggs with roasted potatoes or grits. Served with a croissant.

Continental Breakfast

Choice of Kellogg's brand cereal or hot steel cut oatmeal with raisins and honey. With fresh seasonal fruit, Greek yogurt and a croissant.

Amtrak Signature Buttermilk Pancake Trio
Griddled buttermilk pancakes with breakfast syrup.

Cheese Quesadillas, Eggs & Tomatillo Sauce
Griddled tortillas filled with Monterey Jack cheese, topped with scrambled eggs and tomatillo sauce.

Three Egg Omelet
Made to order omelet with green bell peppers and red onions. Choice of Monterey Jack or Cheddar cheese. Served with a side of tomato salsa, roasted potatoes or grits and a croissant.

Sides & Toppings
Cheddar or Monterey Jack cheese, guacamole, pork sausage, apple maple chicken sausage, applewood smoked bacon.

The sun has risen high enough to light the landscape and the dining car with an eerie haze. Whilst I read the menu I'm taken by surprise as we cross a big river, which looks stunning at this time of the day. I order quesadillas with scrambled eggs. It's a shame I don't have anyone here to compare notes with. I'm scared of grits, I don't really know what a cage free egg is and I'm also a bit apprehensive about hot steel cut oatmeal. My phone is now showing a one bar signal, but from a mast in Mexico. A call via Mexico would cost a lot more than from the US on my airtime plan, so I abandon the idea of calling home and instead get stuck into my quesadilla, which turns out to be a tasty thin cheese toasted taco sandwich.

The journey is stop and start for most of the morning. Around the big curling radius of the track I can see the freight trains approaching. You can sit back and enjoy a cup of coffee in the time it takes for each of these endless lines of wagons to clank past. We eventually reach Alpine, Texas, later in the morning, and there, much against my better judgement, I watch the train pull away without me. They say that you should always try and face your biggest fears, and in railway terms this one was at the top of my list. But Madeline has briefed me on the drill; this is what's known as a 'double spot'. The train is longer than the platform, so it stops, lets passengers at the front of the train disembark, then moves forward and repeats the process for the remainder of the carriages. You might think that it's perfectly okay to watch this from the platform, but to me there is something almost sickening about seeing the train leaving me behind, even momentarily. They say being out of your comfort zone is where you learn new things, so when the engineer blows the horn I wave and watch my carriage leave me behind, with Madeline smiling at me from the open window of the doorway. Managing to hold back my panic, I'm relieved to see the train stop about 100 feet further down the line.

Alpine is the gateway to Big Bend National Park, one of the most remote and least visited parks in the United

States. This is proper cowboy country, and my thoughts turn to the wild west and a time when trains transformed this part of America. The soundtrack in my head is composed by Ennio Morricone. To the chords of 'Once Upon a Time in the West', I strain my eyes trying to spot any cowboys on horseback in the distance.

I'm not going mad, it did once actually happen to me. I took a day trip on the Grand Canyon Railway from Williams, Arizona, to the rim of the canyon. The train was an amazing 1950s diesel-electric locomotive hauling iconic silver Pullman carriages on the daily 64-mile run. The canyon didn't disappoint, and I spent a few hours wandering round its edge and trying not to fall in. You might think that's an obvious goal, but most of the crazy tourists there seemed intent on getting the perfect selfie by jumping up into the gusty air on the unfenced cliff edges. I stayed well back, fending off hungry squirrels and hanging onto my belongings to stop them from blowing over the edge. Tired from all the walking, on the way back to Williams I was just about to nod off for a snooze when I thought I saw something strange out of the corner of my eye. Outside was a gang of men on horseback, racing alongside and easily matching the speed of the train. The man on the first horse wore a lot of tasselled suede, and his face was covered by a scarf. We stared at each other for a few seconds before he pulled out a nickel-plated pistol and waved it in my direction. The train stopped and the gang dismounted and came through the carriages demanding cash and jewellery from the passengers. It turned out that this wasn't a real robbery or even a hallucination, but a show put on by the railway company to keep people occupied on the way home.

I'm thinking of all the western movies I have seen and making a shortlist of my favourites. There are so many to choose from – up until the late 1950s a fifth of Hollywood films were westerns, and eight of the top ten TV shows were cowboy-related. However, the top-drawer films made in Technicolor were eventually replaced by budget films, and then television. In the 1970s I remember hearing the rousing theme tunes to shows like *The High Chaparral* and *Bonanza* that had made it across the pond, later supplemented by 204 episodes of *The Little House on the Prairie*. But my brief love affair with the western didn't start until I had seen *Butch Cassidy and the Sundance Kid* for the first time, quite a few years after its original 1969 release.

I once took the wonderful narrow-gauge tourist train in Colorado that runs between Silverton and Durango. Opened in the 1880s to support the gold and silver mining boom, its 45-mile line runs through the picturesque San Juan mountains. Now, almost every day steam locomotives built in the 1920s haul restored carriages, now painted bright yellow, through the valleys with much tooting and plenty of smoke. As the train climbed higher into the mountains the drop from trackside to the bottom of the valley was no longer a view for the faint-hearted. I had a strange feeling about this place, almost as though the location had been planted deep in my soul. Then it came to me. Butch Cassidy says he'll jump first, but Sundance won't let him, as he can't swim. Butch laughs and tells him not to worry as the fall will probably kill him anyway. When I asked the brakeman, he confirmed that it was the exact spot where that jump was filmed for *Butch Cassidy and the Sundance Kid*. Apparently, Paul Newman and Robert Redford only fell about 5 feet, but some brave stuntmen back in Hollywood did the whole drop. The line was also used for the scenes where Butch and Sundance blew up the Union Pacific Overland Flyer with too much dynamite. It's one of those films that I can watch again and again without ever getting tired of.

It's time to eat, and when I arrive at the end of the dining car John sits me with a man I haven't seen before. We discuss the usual stuff: the weather, the possibility of getting a less than cremated Angus burger from the lunch menu, and our next big stop, El Paso. He nods every now and then and seems to study my every move. After John has dropped him off a rum and soda, he twirls the stirrer in his plastic glass and asks me what I'm doing here. He seems interested to find someone to talk with from outside the United States, and the questions don't stop until he has finished his drink. 'Same again,' he tells John, who replies, in John-speak, 'I got ya!' It turns out that Thomas is a linguist, but when I ask him where he teaches, at first he dodges my question. I learn that he's a body language expert too. No wonder he's been staring at me like that. When he tells me who his employer is, and that he has spent the last 86 weeks learning Arabic, I decide not to ask him any more personal questions.

John pops by to see if I'm having cheesecake or chocolate for dessert, but I tell him I'm going to save myself for dinner. 'Very good, Mr Matthew, I'll see you later,' he says with genuine excitement. I make my excuses and leave Thomas to finish his lunch. I fear I'm acting in a similar way to Basil Fawlty when he meets the psychiatrist in *Fawlty Towers* – but I just want to appear normal, whatever normal might be. Back in my room I prepare for our arrival in El Paso.

El Paso stands on the banks of the Rio Grande, right on the border with Mexico. Not just near the border, but on it. Over the infamous wall is the lawless town of Ciudad Juárez, home of the Juárez cartel and with, until recently, one of the highest violent crime rates in the region. Like any city it has good bits and bad bits, and the views from a train in any city tend to be of the cheaper land. Surveying the place, the term 'bandit country' comes to mind. What I can see over the fence are shanty towns made of mud brick buildings with corrugated iron roofs and huge piles of rubbish. A lot of them are abandoned, as people have moved out to avoid the violence.

Over on my side of the river El Paso looks considerably

more prosperous if a little overly secured by fences and concrete barricades. I have never been here before, but having seen *Traffic* (2000), *Man on Fire* (2004), *No Country for Old Men* (2007) and *Sicario* (2015) I feel that I already know the city quite well. My preconceptions are all about violence and the cross-border movement of drugs, but in reality the city was ranked in the top three safest cities in the United States just a few years ago. Today it's a big well-developed urban hub, with leading industrial tech, education and medical facilities.

I had originally planned to stop here to get a better feel for the place, but the train timetable meant this would have been a three-day stop, and I'm keen to get to Los Angeles on time as I have an appointment to keep. I will just have to park my desire to try a Chile con Queso Steak with Cheesy Bandito Fries until next time.

It's a big station and the platform is long enough to handle the whole train. Strange to think that there is now a parallel universe on board, with passengers from the Texas Eagle serviced by their own dining car, sightseeing lounge and café car. Hopping down onto the platform I seek shade from the beating overhead sun, and find a spot next to a fence some way back from the tracks. I'm joined by a woman in plain clothes. Linda turns out to be an Amtrak auditor, and whilst she enjoys a cigarette I get to ask her about life working on the rails. There isn't much to do other than smoke or sunbathe here, and not being a fan of either I make my way back over to the train. Right on cue, as I do this the engineer blows the horn a couple of times and passengers are ushered back on board. It hasn't been a long stop, but it's always good to get off – an opportunity to touch a real place on the map.

I want to see more of the infamous wall as we head out of town. Eggi is back on the PA in the sightseeing lounge. He points out the Rio Grande, the new wall and the line of the border which everyone seems keen to have a photograph of. He also insists that all passengers join him in a group Yee Ha! as we finally leave Texas and cross into neighbouring New Mexico. We are now 1178 miles from where the Sunset Limited originated – and there's just another 817 miles to LA.

The atmosphere is relaxed here in the sightseeing lounge, other than a couple of women who seem to be arguing about something to do with the last stop. As well as being dressed in lycra they are equipped with all the clichés of 1990s American leisure wear – baseball caps, fanny packs, sweatbands and large cameras suspended around their necks.

Watching our train cross a river that I guess to be the Rio Grande, at first I'm confused. Are we in Mexico now? They assure me we aren't, but are instead just skirting round the edge of the city between the road bridge and the border. Whilst I try to follow the line of the fence to where it becomes the infamous Trumpinspired wall there is a flurry behind me and a passenger I have not seen before runs straight past and through to the next carriage. I can hear the others chatting excitedly about her. Eventually my curiosity gets the better of me, and I ask the lady with the camera, 'What's up?'

The news is that we have just left a passenger behind at El Paso, and the agitated woman is his girlfriend, still on the train, complete with all his luggage and travel documents. He went for a look round the station and didn't make it back on in time. 'They never stop for someone left behind,' the woman nearest to me says, and adds that she has a hire car to drop off in Tucson and if she is charged for returning it late she will sue. This doesn't sound very charitable to me, but I keep this view to myself and listen to the opinions of the rest of the woman's growing audience. It seems about 50/50. The consensus is that if a child had been left it would have been the duty of Amtrak to stop the train. But anyone else can wait for the next train – in this case, not due until three days' time. George Caldwell has a similar problem in *Silver Streak*. He gets thrown off the train twice and has to catch up with it again. He manages this by getting a lift from a farmer in a vintage biplane, and then, with the help of Grover Muldoon, in a stolen police car. But neither of these feel like viable solutions for our missing passenger.

Lost-passenger gossip is going to last until at least dinner tonight, possibly breakfast. It turns out that the missing passenger's partner was on her way to find the conductor to beg him to stop the train. They were headed to LA this way as he doesn't like flying. He's left all his documentation and money on the train, so now the only alternative is for her to get off somewhere in New Mexico and hire a car. Except she can't drive. I feel for them both. All for a packet of cigarettes. I nearly made the same mistake once, and have been paranoid about keeping my train in sight ever since. I still have nightmares about it, though.

The experience in the sightseeing carriage gives me an idea for a new television show. A rail-based soap opera with characters having everyday rail-based problems. The social centre is in the café car or the dining car. Occasionally people get off and new mysterious characters join the cast. The BBC used this concept in a TV series called *Triangle* in the early 1980s. Set on a North Sea ferry, it lasted nearly three series before being cancelled. It was possibly one of the worst shows ever made. I make a note to mention this to someone in LA. I'll work out the plot to the first episode in bed later on.

In the middle of the observation car is a small serving area made of polished steel, but from what I've seen so far, Amtrak doesn't seem to use these any more. Instead, you take the stairs down to the café bar underneath. It's the place where anyone on board can get a microwaved meal or a cold beer. On this train the staff call it John's Place. Madeline says that I look a lot like John, so I decide to go and meet my doppelgänger. Hanging on to the slender rail to steady myself as I descend the steps, I emerge on the lower level. Apart from a few seats the carriage is taken up by banks of chillers and racks carrying a huge variety of snacks and drinks. At the far end of the carriage is a bar where I'm greeted by the man himself and Eggi, his partner in crime. Eggi is cracking the jokes and making the announcements on the PA this shift whilst John does the heavy lifting. I can tell that they are both a bit sad about the stranded passenger. I hadn't expected that. It seems to have lowered their mood from the normal level of mad as a box of frogs to just zany and fun.

I choose a craft beer and a cheese plate, and John fits them into a little cardboard tray so that I can carry them back up the stairs. The mood in the sightseeing lounge mellows as the sun dips slowly behind the mountaintops. Thoughts of El Paso have been left behind, replaced by the wonder and awe of the huge skies of Arizona. I finally spot the lady I'd met in the station in Houston and join her for a chat. Her name is Veronica, and she looks quite well for someone who has been in a coach seat for the last 24 hours. As we watch the sunset over a beer we compare notes on our journey so far. The lounge becomes a planetarium, and she points out Orion, but I can't see it, with the train curving around the tracks in the bottom of the steep valley.

Dinner, as always, is convivial and I enjoy a signature

steak with a glass of red wine whilst listening to the plans of some fellow travellers. The majority of citizens in the United States appear to discount the possibility of ever taking a long-distance train, but there is a small minority who embrace it. It's a nice mix of people, mainly retired people who are not in a hurry and like seeing the sights along the route, and younger people who are trying to have a travel experience on the cheap. But I can also see the emergence of a new class of Amtrak passenger, those who are trying to reduce their carbon footprint and have therefore stopped flying. Then there are the pro train travellers love it so much that nothing gives them more pleasure than swapping notes on particular routes and places along the way. These are America's hard core railfans. Around the table this evening we have probably covered all the main Amtrak routes and services. The dining car is closing for the evening, and as we will be arriving before breakfast I have to say goodbye to John and Eggi. I'm surprised how attached to them I have become in just 48 hours. I wish I could bring them with me onto the next trip. All the staff have been great, but John has melted my heart. I have a fantasy that he takes over a large company or even a government and starts running things with his own set of values. What a place to work that would be.

Because of the delays, our arrival into Yuma is now scheduled for 12.49am rather than 3.10pm, so I'm not going to see much of it. I have never been a big fan of Russell Crowe, but the 2007 adaptation of Elmore

Leonard's 1953 story, *3.10 to Yuma*, is a pretty good film, perhaps almost as good as my go-to modern western, *Unforgiven* (1992). Much like *Butch Cassidy and the Sundance Kid*, it's also in my sweet spot of westerns featuring the railroad. *Yuma* was actually mainly shot in Santa Fe, a place I'm going to visit later in my adventure.

In the morning I wake up before my alarm, knowing that our arrival into LA is scheduled for 5.35am. I have always found that I wake up before I need to, and I think I have read somewhere that this is a natural human condition. I fell asleep with the blinds open, and my view now is of low-level hacienda-style houses and a jungle of concrete drainage channels in the pre-dawn glow.

The empty concrete rivers are familiar to me from my childhood. I remember hiding behind the sofa in our lounge as I watched a swarm of giant irradiated ants emerging from the New Mexico desert and making their nest in a tunnel right there. I didn't see the whole film, as it scared me even more than the cybermen in *Doctor Who* at the time; instead I chose to remain behind the sofa until Basil Brush appeared a bit later on. *Them!* was shot in 1954, and it's a classic big bug film from a time when the United States was unsure about the nuclear world. Fortunately, the good guys manage to kill the ants with flamethrowers and sub-machine guns, so everyone could sleep soundly.

But if you showed most people a photograph of these

drainage channels today they would remember them from a more recent film. In 1991 James Cameron directed the sequel to *The Terminator*. One of the highest-grossing box office films ever made, it catapulted Arnold Schwarzenegger to superstar. Travelling back in time, he must protect his future leader, John Connor, from the T-1000 Terminator sent by Skynet, a vicious killing machine made of a mimetic polyalloy that can take on the appearance of anything it encounters. Once Arnie has recovered John, he attempts to escape from the T-1000 on a Harley Davidson Fat Boy down one of these drainage channels. The leather-clad biker look, complete with shades and a shotgun, is an iconic image from the film. In my opinion it's one of only a handful of sequels that are possibly better than the original film, along with *The Godfather Part II* – but definitely not *Aliens*.

I don't have long to consider other possible candidates for film sequels, as we pull into Union Station before I have managed to pack up. I like to be organised well before arrival and, caught out by this, I go into a bit of an OCD-induced panic. I needn't have worried, though; the train isn't going anywhere and there is plenty of time. Madeline is on the platform with a huddle of the crew. They wish me well, and Madeline points me in the direction of the luggage reclaim.

Even though it's not even 6am, the station has a hum of activity, with local commuters as well as long-distance passengers beginning to fill the hallways and platforms.

You might imagine that Union Station would be a slightly dangerous place, especially in the dark. If you have seen *Boyz n the Hood* or *Straight Outta Compton* you might even be prepared for a gang war – but nothing could be further from reality. The station is calm and clean. It's a beautiful structure, built in the 1930s using a combination of architectural styles. The marble floors and wooden-beamed ceilings surrounded by courtyards and gardens give the place a peaceful feel. Off the main concourse I find a room with a baggage belt and wait for my bag, along with a small crowd of other bleary passengers. Across the room a couple of police officers in distinctive black LAPD outfits look on.

Silver Streak

Chapter Eight
Dogtown

By the time I have managed to find a taxi the coolness of the early morning has been replaced by the heat of a cloudless sky and the microclimate of a big city. The little yellow and green car that has picked me up weaves around a few blocks before finding the freeway down to Santa Monica and the traffic of the early morning rush hour. Over my shoulder is my first view of the LA skyline, and it's just as it appeared in the opening credits to *The A-Team*, 'a crack commando unit sent to prison by a military court for a crime they didn't commit'. Surviving as soldiers of fortune in the Los Angeles underground, the unit was made up of Colonel 'Hannibal' Smith, Lieutenant Templeton Peck or 'Faceman', Captain 'Howling Mad' Murdoch, and Sergeant B.A. Baracus, better known as 'Mr T'. I point out the skyline to the driver and try to engage in a conversation with him about the show. I always felt George Peppard was a strange choice as Colonel Smith, but he needed the money, and

James Coburn had turned the part down. My Mexican driver hasn't got an opinion on this and doesn't know where I might find them today. Instead he wants to talk about the British royal family and asks me to pass his best regards on to the Queen. He tells me his name is Jesus. Jesus sends no special message, only his best wishes. I make a note of this in my journal and wonder what Her Majesty will think.

Advertising hoardings always give me a clue about the sort of life that people might lead in in places that I visit. On this freeway it's mainly lawyers looking for injury claims and religions looking for new recruits. I love the way American advertising can be so direct. Not boringly assuring corporate signs, but pictures of real people with personal messages of how they will save you. Even estate agents have signs with the photograph of the broker selling the house.

Jesus does his best to weave in and out of the almost stationary traffic, but we have to queue to peel off the Pasadena Freeway and onto the highway down to Santa Monica. He tries a few manoeuvres that fill me with shame, but I'm sure they are standard procedure for taxi drivers here in LA. I don't actually mind the interruption of our progress at this point, as we are at a film location of particular poignancy for fans of violent crime films: underneath us right now is the spot where Michael Mann shot the armoured truck robbery scene in his 1995 film, *Heat*. A remake of his original TV film, *Heat* is stunning to watch, and really nails the style of crime drama he is famous for from television, like *Miami Vice*. Bringing the talents of Robert De Niro and Al Pacino together in his film also ensured that it became a huge commercial success. Films this good this can even make the drab concrete of the interstate underpasses feel exciting.

Budget hotels are expensive here in Santa Monica, and looking around in my new home I can't see many visible frills. When I ask the man behind the reception counter if I can check in, he has to steady himself to avoid laughing. Check-in is from 3pm, he tells me, with his best customer-friendly face of polite pity. I tell him that I've already paid for the room for the night, knowing that I might need to sleep for a couple of hours after my early arrival. Now which one of us is the fool? He hands me a room key and, as if trying to make amends, shows me through to the breakfast room, where I find a seat by the huge windows that look out onto the street.

Having only just got used to the code of the all-American breakfast, I find things a little strange here. The room is dominated by three industrial-sized waffle machines, and I'm intimidated by them as I have never made a waffle before. Instead I opt for a cup of coffee from the choice of three blends and wait until I can watch someone else make a waffle and take some notes. A couple of kids take pity on me after a few minutes and show me the ropes. The scariest part is not the production of the waffle itself, but post-production with the range of toppings on offer. In what sick world do you have *waffle toppings* at this hour? I let my teachers choose them for me, and head back to my table with whipped cream, fruit, and hundreds & thousands on my plate – and it's not yet 7am.

The street looks equally unfamiliar. People pass by on roller skates, hoverboards and little electric scooters. Some even spot my comedy waffles and wave. Women carrying a mixture of dogs, smoothies and children jog past. But there is also an underclass that is very visible here. The combination of a warm climate, a beach and more permissive laws than the rest of Los Angeles have made the town a mecca for those living on the fringes of society. Welcome to Santa Monica, Matthew.

I wake from a refreshingly deep sleep around lunchtime, and once I have sorted myself out I stroll down Colorado Avenue to say hello to the Pacific Ocean. Santa Monica Pier dominates the view from the beach. If you ever saw Steven Spielberg's *1941*, or films from the Rocky or Beverly Hills Cop franchises, then you will recognise it immediately. The warm sunshine and gentle breeze put me in a good mood. I have no reason to hurry, and enjoy wandering along with all the other people that didn't bring a skateboard.

I made my first skateboard from a rough plank of wood and pair of old roller skates nailed on underneath in the long hot summer of 1976. It was a deathtrap, but I had to wait until Christmas until I got hold of a real but rather nasty orange polypropylene board. After having several near-death accidents, I was also given pads and a helmet to improve my chances of survival. But while I was mastering simple tic-tacs and bunny hops, a gang of kids known as the Zephyr Skateboard Team were becoming famous in Santa Monica and Venice Beach, a place known in the surf culture of the time as Dogtown. In the concrete of empty swimming pools in the summer drought they perfected surf-inspired moves that I could only dream of performing without needing a trip to my local hospital's A&E. In 2001 a film called *Dogtown and Z-Boys* was released, written by Stacy Peralta and Craig Stecyk, telling the story of this subculture. It's narrated by Sean Penn, and the soundtrack rocks.

Unsurprisingly, the shops on the pier are packed with fairly trashy LA-based tourist merchandise. Amongst the ubiquitous brightly coloured Venice Beach Lifeguard, I Love LA and Lakers shirts are just a few with the iconic Route 66 logo. Highway 66, or the Mother Road, connects Chicago with LA on a legendary 2448-mile road trip that finishes in Santa Monica. Today most of the original route has been replaced by the interstate highway, but some sections of the historic route and the signs are now protected, and it's a big tourism draw. I'll be headed back in the direction of Chicago on a train called the Southwest Chief. This must make it the Route 66 of trains.

It's great to wander around with time to stop to watch the performers, the musicians and the hustlers. Today I'm more than content to be a tourist. I spot an amusement arcade which piques my interest. With the rise of home entertainment these places are no longer places for kids but shrines for retro gamers, the children of the 70s and 80s. Inside, vintage machines line the walls, winking, beeping and playing their theme music, competing for the attention of passing worshippers. All my favourites are here – Pac-Man, Donkey Kong, Pole Position and OutRun – even After Burner. But the machine that catches my eye is very different, one that I have never seen in a Brighton or Blackpool arcade before. Inside the tall glass case sits a bearded man with a yellow turban and a black waistcoat over an elaborate golden gown. In front of him is a crystal ball. He holds a wand in one hand. 'I am Zoltar, the great gypsy,' he says to me. 'I can see your fortune. Come, let Zoltar tell you more.' Deciding it's worth a dollar to know if I'm going to miss any of my trains, I eagerly feed a banknote into the machine and await my fortune. The simple percussive sounds of a xylophone, a slight pause for effect, and he says to me 'The great Zoltar sees much happiness ahead for you,' and a little card pops out underneath the great man which contains something similar to an astrological reading. It all looks good, and nowhere does he mention missing my train or getting left behind. I thank him and wander on down the pier towards the ocean. It takes me a couple of minutes, but I eventually figure out my strange familiarity with the machine. It was central to the plot in the 1988 film *Big*. That's the one where David Moscow, the junior version of Tom Hanks's Josh Baskin, made a wish to be big to a Zoltar machine. The film wasn't set here, but at a carnival site in New Jersey. The machine was identical, though, and that is because a Nevada-based animatronic company has been licensed to reproduce fortune-telling machines with the same name since 1997.

Old men wrinkled by the sun are fishing at the end of the pier. Up the beach one way are the cliffs behind Malibu, and as far away in the other direction, the yacht masts of the port at Long Beach. No one seems to be catching very much, but that's not the important thing here. It's a social activity, and a few buckets of salty water and a pier fishing rod is the perfect cover story for a good day out with your friends. Right here in the 1985 film *Fletch*, the actor Chevy Chase was on a cover story of a different nature – as Fletch, an undercover reporter for the LA Times, who uncovers a drug-running ring on the beaches of Los Angeles. A number of scenes were shot under the pier, beneath my very feet. It became a bit of a cult film with Chevy Chase at his very best, and a sequel titled *Fletch Lives* has been in development for more than 20 years. Chevy is in his late 70s now, so I hope they make it soon.

It's the weekend, and Santa Monica and the seafront are bustling with middle-class families and parties of college kids escaping LA for some sun and sand. From my vantage point of a park bench on Ocean Avenue I can watch everything that's going on. A group of performers are setting up in a prime spot above the pier. It's a masterclass in getting people to want to wait to watch a show. The group are called the LA Breakers, and their MC tells the growing crowd that they are world famous. I'm drawn to get a place in the audience before it gets too busy. The warm-up guy with the microphone scans his crowd and picks on me. 'Where you from?' he asks. I consider explaining that I live in a quiet corner of West Sussex, but decide instead to tell him that I live in London. It's usually easier, as most people know roughly where London is. He uses the moment of trans-Atlantic friendship to introduce the team – they are from Puerto Rico, Mexico, Thailand, but mainly south-central LA. His eyes narrow as he tries to work me out. 'What do you do?' he asks, 'You look like you're undercover.' I suspect being described as undercover isn't a compliment, but I'm not rising to it. His attention then turns to finding volunteers for the show, and I'm off the hook, having done my bit. The crowd now know me as the undercover Englishman.

The Breakers start their act, popping and jumping about a bit, spinning on various parts of their body to beats from the portable sound system. The MC introduces the tallest of the group. He's called the human elastic band, and today he's going to jump over five members of the audience. He's fit and supremely flexible, but I still fear this might end in tears. It's the climax of the show, and the moment when as much money as possible can be extracted from the audience. I can't believe how far they go to hustle and embarrass people into making bigger donations, but it's all part of the show. When there's no more money coming in, he gives the signal to the elastic band, who runs in from the street and somersaults over volunteers to the amazement of the crowd. Then it's all over, as the Breakers want a new crowd with pockets of fresh dollars.

Down the road just a block from the pier is the Ocean View Hotel. You might not think too much of it as a place to stay if you haven't watched the highly acclaimed TV show *Goliath*. This is down-and-out lawyer Billy McBride's home, played by the excellent Billy Bob Thornton. You can see the door to his room at the end of the second floor from the street. Next door is the dive bar, Chez Jay, that also features in the show. It's a well-known local landmark and something of a celebrity hang-out, so I decide to have a drink there. Maybe I might meet someone who could commission a show out of my rail-and-beer lifestyle? This was once the home to the Rat Pack, the Beach Boys, and even Marilyn Monroe, who preferred table 10. Even Richard Burton and Peter Sellers were once known to frequent the place.

Inside I have to let my eyes adjust to the dim interior before finding somewhere to sit down. It's almost as though people are hiding in here. The bar isn't quite where I think it's going to be, the result of watching too many episodes of *Goliath*. Lucky to find a seat at the bar, I order a margarita. What has become of me? I just figure this is the right drink for someone looking to land a film deal. The man next to me introduces himself. Sadly, Todd isn't a movie director, but like me is also looking to meet someone here today. He produces his phone, which has a dating app running. We review a few potential matches and he gives me his top tips for dating in Dogtown. I have many questions that I would like to ask, but I decide not to go down the rabbit hole. Apparently, this a good place to meet first dates; Blake Edwards and Julie Andrews first met here. After a couple of drinks and too many peanuts, I make my excuses and head back to my hotel, which looks quite smart after the Ocean View.

Chapter Nine
The Rockford Files

British television was pretty limited in the late 1970s. Hours of test card and Open University at night and a diet of dull soap operas during most of the day. The weekend was where the networks spent most of their limited budgets. ITV was regarded as mainly satanic by the senior members of my family, which left me, as an enquiring-minded schoolboy, just two channels to choose from. I had to be protected at all costs from the tomfoolery of *Tiswas* and *Magpie*, ITV's answer to *Blue Peter*, but where the presenters spoke in regional accents that were not viewed as good for my education. Children's television was shown in concentrated bursts around teatime during the week, where *Blue Peter*, *Grange Hill*, *John Craven's Newsround* and *Rhubarb & Custard* were broadcast as a single set-piece lump before the evening news.

Saturday mornings were a bit different, and were considerably improved if I had permission to watch *Space 1999* on the other channel. And that was the problem. *Space 1999* showed *Doctor Who* up for the underbudgeted and overstretched show that it really was. *Space 1999* had big budgets, as Gerry Anderson had tied up with Lew Grade and ITC in the United States. British TV just couldn't compete in the age of *Star Wars* – ironically, a film mainly made at Elstree Studios, just up the road from where I lived.

Towards the end of the decade American programmes started to be shown a lot more on British television. The BBC gave up trying to compete directly, and supplemented its well-worn classics with all sorts of shows from across the pond. Elder members of my family began to write letters of complaint to the director general, but I secretly loved it. You had to take the rough with the smooth, though. *The Waltons* and *The Little House on the Prairie* provided never-ending sugar-coated family TV. *Happy Days* seemed fun but was still cool – but there was more exciting stuff, often a bit later on, if that wasn't past your bedtime. *The Six Million Dollar Man* was essential viewing, along with shows like *Charlie's Angels* and *Hawaii Five-O*. But the pinnacle of my evening viewing habits was a programme shown on a Tuesday night just after 8pm about a man who lived in a mobile home on a beachside parking lot in Malibu. His name was Jim Rockford, and you could leave your message for him after the tone on his Dictaphone 660.

He drove a Pontiac Firebird Esprit. Cars were mainly terrible in Britain at this time, and Jim's Firebird seemed very exotic, more a supercar than an everyday vehicle. It certainly bore no resemblance to my family's canary yellow Ford Escort 1.2 Popular, lacking even wing mirrors and a radio.

Jim's life on the beach, solving cases, fishing with his dad and generally hanging out in the Californian sun, seemed amazing compared to our existence in the British recession of the period. It was also noted as an adult programme that I was officially allowed to watch, as long as I didn't start saying American words like 'yeah' instead of 'yes' at the dinner table. Back then, 'yeah' was a slippery slope. If it wasn't nipped in the bud, the feeling was that I would become an unemployable dropout in a matter of hours.

Everything about *The Rockford Files* was different from a British TV drama. It had a brilliant catchy Mike Post theme tune, cool quick framed shots of locations across downtown Los Angeles, and of course James Garner wearing shades driving his copper-coloured Firebird down the freeway in the hot sun. At the end of the title sequence an answer machine message would always be played, even though it usually had nothing to do with the plot of each episode. Rockford wasn't a typical private eye. A once-convicted criminal, he rarely carried his gun. He looked a bit scruffy, and tried to avoid getting into trouble. You could buy his services for $200 a day. The show had been manufactured around James Garner after the success of cowboy show *Maverick*. It was in many ways a modern-day version of the same show, and it was a huge success all over the world. They made a total of 123 episodes between 1974 and 1980. There were movie spin-offs too, but not until some years later, as Garner had a long-running legal dispute over money with Universal, the studio which had made them.

So now, more than 40 years since the last episode was filmed, I want to connect with Jim and his life in Malibu. I need to find Jim Rockford to thank him for getting me through the dark evenings of Britain in the late 1970s. My search reveals that his home was in a small place off the Pacific Coast Highway called Paradise Cove, about 20 miles from my base in Santa Monica. His address was 29 Cove Road. At first, I try calling his number (555-2368) but unsurprisingly it turns out to be a fake one that was also used in several other shows and had been specially invented by the telephone company. Very sadly, my hero James Garner died of a heart attack in 2014, but I hope I might still find something of his spirit and legacy there.

I'm lucky enough to have a friend in town who has agreed to help in my Rockford quest. Josh Weinstein lives in Santa Monica where he works as a television writer and producer best known for his work on shows like *The Simpsons*. Only in LA could you have a friend who does that kind of thing. More importantly to me, he also happens to be a huge railfan, which is how we first came across each other. Josh remembers the show well, and thinks he knows where Paradise Cove is. Navigating through the downtown blocks, we emerge onto the Pacific Coast Highway and turn northwards in the direction of Malibu. Highway 1 runs for over 650 miles from south of LA to north of San Francisco, and the views out over the ocean are at times spectacular. Josh knows this stretch well, as it takes us past his old office and the houses of a few celebrities that if I mentioned them you would accuse me of name-dropping. It's home to a few fictional characters too. Miles Dyson's house from *Terminator 2: Judgment Day* is just up here in the hills. No gunfire was allowed without special permission when filming so as not to scare the horses. How do you tell Arnold Schwarzenegger not to fire his guns, I wonder? – he's a Terminator. Charlie Harper's house from *Two and a Half Men* is set here too, but the show was actually all filmed in the studio. His home is supposed to be on Colony Road close to Malibu Pier – if it were, he would be sandwiched somewhere between Leonardo DiCaprio, Cindy Crawford and Ridley Scott. Further up the highway is Neptune's Nest, the diner location from the original *Point Break* film where Keanu Reeves's Johnny Utah tries to chat up Lori Petty, playing the role of Tyler Endicott. Josh does a brilliant job as my guide, pointing out interesting and infamous places along the way.

The haze burns away and it's a clear sunny day with just a slight ocean mist. I'm wearing the coolest clothes I have with me as a rail adventurer, which to be honest are not really Malibu cool. My sunglasses have the effect of saturating the colours, making everything look like it's still in a hit 1970s TV show. We might not be in a Firebird, but the coffee holders are better in Josh's car, and the air conditioning works really well too. We pass under green highway signs indicating the turn-offs to places I've heard of but never visited. Eventually we reach a sign for Cove Road and head down to the beach. We are not the only people to have the idea of a weekend lunch in Paradise Cove, but we're probably the only people here because of our fondness for *The Rockford Files*. Safely parked, we sip on artisan coffee whilst working out where everything from the show would have been positioned here. In the spirit of modern-day super sleuths and Indiana Jones-inspired archaeologists, we find a small plaque hidden in a hedge under a palm tree. It's not the Holy Grail, but it is of historical importance to us. There is a black & white photo of the trailer he lived in, a picture of Jim with his car, and another with him and his dad Rocky (played by Noah Beery, Jr) on the pier. What's a little sad is that a few metres away there is a much better positioned sign proclaiming this was the very spot where the Beach Boys photographed the cover to their 1962 album, *Surfin' Safari*. It might have been the birth of the California Sound, but I prefer the theme tune to *The Rockford Files*. Mike Post was a legend, and his theme tunes were ubiquitous in my childhood televisual enjoyment.

Waddling through the hot sand and onto the rickety old pier you get a great perspective of the cove. Rocky isn't here any more, and no one's fishing here today; it's just us and the seagulls. Paradise Cove used to be a fishing mecca with hundreds of fishers buying bait, renting boats and heading onto this pier every day. What I didn't realise, though, was that long before *The Rockford Files* it was already a well-used location for television shows portraying Malibu as a beach community for surfers, sailors and fishers. Today it looks tired and run down, but thankfully authentic and untouched by the development that has enveloped much of the coastline.

The Paradise Cove Beach Café is buzzing, but the maître d' promises he will fix something for us in a few minutes. Waiting in the bar, I admire the walls, covered with old photos, the sort that you only wish you could find out a bit more of their context. Pictures of fit, smiling men with fishing rods and boats. They don't seem to have a care in the world. I wonder what they did, and if they're still around today. If their lives were based around fishing from this beach they were definitely on to a good thing.

Our table is very familiar to me. It's identical to one that Jim Rockford sits in when he's lunching with his dad or his latest love interest. Except that in *The Rockford Files* the restaurant was called the Tonga Lei Lounge or Don the Beachcomber's Lounge. The light is dim in the front room, but the sun streams in from our view of the beach, so I keep my sunglasses on. Not to look cool, but to protect my eyes. Over fried fish po'boys we discuss all things rail and what's up with Amtrak. Josh confirms my suspicion that most Americans think that travel by train is a mad idea. They often have an Amtrak horror story to tell, one of being delayed for days and never reaching their destination. Stories of the experience are passed from generation to generation and embellished at every Thanksgiving dinner. It's reinforced in the movies too. No wonder Amtrak has an uncomfortable relationship with Hollywood. They always want to make films about trains breaking down, trains blowing up, or trains crashing, never trains arriving on time or being comfortable. For a man living the dream in LA, Josh has his own favourite destination: Wales and its steam-powered railways. He'd love to live in the countryside. The grass is always greener on the other side of the fence. Sat here in the Malibu sunshine, I can't quite understand why anyone would want to live anywhere else.

Back outside in the car park I discover a dark secret of Paradise Cove. The producers of the Lethal Weapon films relocated Martin Riggs' trailer home from Playa del Rey to Paradise Cove in the fourth film of the franchise. I'm not sure if it's good or bad karma that Mel Gibson and James Garner live similar lifestyles in the very same spot but twenty years apart. There could have been a great convergence scene where Martin Riggs discovers Jim Rockford's Dictaphone 600 and picks up his unsolved cases. Maybe Jim could have left his revolver and sunglasses hidden under the hatch that Mel Gibson's dog uses to go in and out of the trailer?

On the way back to Santa Monica we stop at Malibu Pier. Just parking here costs as much as our lunch, but Josh has worked out that the opening credits of *The Rockford Files* were filmed here rather than at Paradise Cove. The sign pronounces it as the 'Malibu Sport Fishing Pier – live bait and charter boats', and it's a lot busier here than Paradise Cove. Blink and you'd miss it, but he's right. It's the shot where Jim is fishing with Rocky, who is pointing out something in the distance. God bless Noah Beery Jr. Josh and I try to recreate this image – but we have no fishing rods and we can't agree which one of us is to be Jim and which Rocky. We have to explain this to the Japanese couple who have agreed to take the photograph and seem concerned for our mental well-being.

Before we leave the pier, I notice the restaurant at the end of the pier and its vague familiarity. I have to walk right up to it before I can work it out. This is the restaurant at the end of *Taken 2*, when Bryan Mills, played by Liam Neeson, buys his family a milkshake and promises not to shoot his daughter's new boyfriend. I was a big fan of the original, but it turned out to be one of those franchises that didn't improve with the sequels. Bryan Mills must be one of the unluckiest film characters of all time, possibly only beaten by John McLane in the *Die Hard* movies. Every family outing turns into an organised crime bloodbath.

I could spend quite a lot more time here were it not for my dwindling bank balance and the lack of a good skateboard. I also have a forward reservation on my next train, the Southwest Chief, tomorrow afternoon. So on my final evening I make the most of the hedonistic and cocktail-infused nightlife of LA. My only disappointment during my stay here, other than the lack of a television deal, is that I haven't been able to meet up with Rod Stewart. This isn't because I'm the biggest-ever fan of his music, but because he owns an enormous model railway which he has been building for years in the attic of his Beverly Hills mansion. It would have been a tall order to organise, so I'll have to try again on another occasion. Putting this small setback behind me, I'm really excited about what lies ahead.

Chapter Ten
Silver Streak

The driver of my taxi back to Union Station is a hungry Armenian. He's impressed that I manage to guess his nationality from his accent. When I tell him that I have recently been to Yerevan, he turns the radio down and calls his wife. I have a short but lively conversation with her, and passing the phone back he offers to share his bag of dried apricots with me, which turn out to be absolutely delicious. He shows me some photos of his daughter's wedding as we speed along the Santa Monica Freeway.

Amtrak staff can be amazingly helpful, and then just when you start to take this for granted, things can sometimes go wrong. I follow the instructions at the check-in area and stand in a short queue signposted 'Southwest Chief'. When I reach the counter the woman behind it glances at my ticket – 'Sleepers over there,'

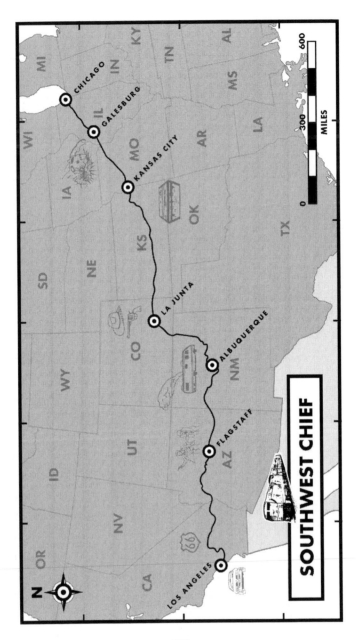

SOUTHWEST CHIEF

she says, pointing to the counter next door. Having retraced my steps and joined another lane without a sign for the Chief, I'm confronted by another woman who seems equally unhappy to see me. She weighs my bag with a look that says she hopes it is going to be overweight. 49.6 lbs. Visibly disappointed by this, she is unaware that I have pre-weighed my luggage to avoid any such confrontation. She scribbles something on my ticket and hands it back, together with a luggage tag. Without looking at me she points vaguely in the direction of the lounge, hoping I will disappear. But the problem is that I'm a bit of a worrier: whenever I get onto a plane I have a habit of wanting to see my bag with its tag on before letting it get taken away on the baggage belt. Today it's harder as there is a high counter and a screen between where I'm standing and my bag, and I have to peer over her. My bag is tagged to go to Chicago, but my next destination is actually Albuquerque. We straighten things out and the bag is retagged. It's all my fault, apparently.

Things are a lot better upstairs in the Metropolitan Lounge. It's full, and the staff seem stretched, but they know exactly what's going on. I'm learning to like this moment in an Amtrak journey. All you have to do is relax and wait for boarding to be called. I wish it could be a bit more glamorous, though. This is the start of the Silver Streak journey; the Southwest Chief is one of Amtrak's most iconic routes. But here in the lounge there is no chance to buy a cocktail or flirt with other passengers in the way Gene Wilder might have done. At best it's coffee in a paper cup, or a bottle of water. That's a long way from the halcyon days of the route, when this was the only civilised way to travel the 2265 miles between LA and Chicago.

The Southwest Chief was originally called the Super Chief. In the 1930s it was the flagship train of the Atchison, Topeka and Santa Fe Railway. Back then they ran the train with all sleeper carriages, and a second train called the El Capitan ran regular seated coaches. When Amtrak took over the route in the 1970s, Santa Fe made them de-brand the Super Chief as it was no longer meeting the service standards that passengers knew the train so well for. It became known as the Southwest Limited. It wasn't until 1984 that service standards had been restored enough for it to get the famous name back, when it became the Southwest Chief. Like many Amtrak lounges, the walls here are adorned with all sorts of memorabilia. I particularly like some of the posters for the Chief. One has an American Indian with an elaborate feather headdress. 'The Chief is still the Chief' it exclaims. Next to it is an illustration of the pleasure dome on top of the sightseeing lounge. Affluent, well-dressed couples look out at the night sky. The men, dressed in lounge suits, wear moustaches and smoke cigarettes. The headline is 'Top of the Super Chief – Next to the Stars!'

Most of the passengers in the lounge have requested a Red Cap service today, so as there are only a couple of buggies available they get transported to the train in batches. The handful of us left behind are invited to make our own way – across the concourse, down into the subway under the tracks and up the stairs to reach the platform. The Chief is backing in just as we arrive. I wave at the fireman looking out of the back of the approaching tail end carriage, but he completely ignores me. He's far too cool to wave, plus he's on the walkie-talkie to the engineer.

When I reach my carriage, I tell the attendant that I'll be opposite her up top, a coded signal to indicate that I know where I'm going, my roomette being number two, opposite the attendants' room. Toni smiles a bright-white-tooth smile and says 'All right number two. Welcome aboard!' Settling in and unpacking my day bag, I find something that I'd forgotten all about. When I arrived in LA a few days ago I spotted that the ticket desk had some children's entertainment packs. The sort of thing you get on an airplane, but instead of a jumbo jet, a cardboard cutout model of a Genesis locomotive and a Junior Conductor's hat. The ticket agent let me have one with a look of mild concern. Now it takes me about five minutes to build the model engine, and I proudly place it on the little table in front of me. I secretly hope that someone might pop by to appraise my technique and award me a gold star or whatever they use in these parts to indicate good work.

Toni likes to run a tidy sleeper and she makes a long and borderline dictatorial speech on the PA. It all sounds perfectly reasonable, and sad that it even needs to be said, but of course there are some people out there that just don't care. Once we are under way I make my dinner reservation and take a stroll through to the sightseeing carriage. Downstairs in the café I meet Michael and Chris, who are running the show. My greeting causes some confusion, though. When I simply say, 'Good evening, chaps,' Michael, mistaking me for a member of Village People after some leather, points out to me that they don't sell chaps. 'Just what you see, sir,' he says. But with this sorted out they serve me a cold bottle of Sierra Nevada beer. I run into more difficulty asking for a packet of crisps. 'Like Cheetos,' I tell them. I should have asked for chips.

The evening runs smoothly as we cross California headed for Arizona. I'm happy just writing my journal, but Toni wants me to go to bed. She's keen to go off shift, so we agree she will turn my bed down just before we arrive at Barstow at 21.56, or 9.56pm as the Amtrak timetable says. I'm not sure why the US has avoided the 24-hour clock outside its military, as the 12-hour system can be really confusing. But not as confusing to me as dates written in the month, day, year order. When she comes to do what's needed I wait outside in the corridor and peer into her room. It's almost identical to my roomette, except it's a bit of a mess and above the door on one side is the tell-tale range of lights and switches. 'You've got all the buttons in there,' I tell her. 'I hear you, sweetheart,' she says from somewhere underneath my bed.

I decide to get some fresh air, and step off the Chief when we stop at Barstow. It's a big hub for both rail and road, and the stop is long enough for me to take a stroll. Most people have already turned in for the night, and when I return to the door of carriage 0430 there is only one other passenger on the platform. Most Americans I meet seem to have one killer fact about themselves to drop into quick conversations with strangers. It's much more fun than the usual set-piece 'How are you?', 'I'm okay,' back in Britain. Angela, on the platform, has a good one. She's on her way back to a place called Lancaster, where she lives with her husband. He used to fly the Space Shuttle. When I remark on the name of her town, I discover she doesn't know what an Avro Lancaster is, or even who the dam busters were. I do my best to explain, but Toni ushers us back onto the train before I get to the good bit about Barnes Wallis and the little wooden aiming device for dropping the bouncing bomb. It's also an epic film, of course, and I really hope that the planned Peter Jackson remake never happens. There seem to be so many remakes of original films out there, and many are not nearly as good as the originals. In Hollywood they call them reboots, an expression I don't much like either. On the spot at Barstow, I can't think of a single one. *The Dam Busters* was the most popular film of 1955 in Great Britain, a time when it still had a film industry. Legend has it that it was also the inspiration for the Death Star trench run in the original *Star Wars* film, a nice connection given that it was also filmed in England.

If I add it all up I must have spent months, if not years, on sleeper trains trying to get a good night's sleep. Conditions of sleepers are normally split into three main types: those that are too hot and those that are too cold are the most common, and then the rarer carriage where the temperature is just right. Most Amtrak trains run slightly cold, which I much prefer to being too hot. You can always put more blankets on, but there is nothing much you can do about being too hot with the windows sealed shut. Unlike on some other railways, there is no secret Amtrak key to open them either. Their design takes into account constant climatic change and the need for a good air conditioning system. Carriage 0430 is a bit older than some Superliner sleepers I have been on, and its system seems to cycle between cold and warm and then cold again, but mostly cold. In the confinement of my little bed, I sleep in two positions to cope with this fluctuation – the 'sausage roll' when it's cold, and the 'walk like an Egyptian' whenever it turns temporarily too hot. I hear a few passengers grumble about this during the night, but there is no local carriage temperature adjustment; it is either on or off – and off would be a disaster. I once saw a lady on the Sunset Limited produce a roll of cling film and use it to cover up all the air vents in her roomette. That's a pro tip if you'd rather be hot than cold.

For some reason I can't sleep, and I rise early the following morning with a slightly thick head. The coffee station is right outside my room, and as I help myself to a cup of steaming java Toni passes by with a big bundle of bedding. 'Morning, Englishman,' she says. I smile at her and wonder if this is a putdown or a compliment. I think she's just being friendly. I've missed the early morning stop at Flagstaff and there's only one other quick stop this morning before the Chief is due to reach Albuquerque just before lunchtime. But now it's only 6.30 in the morning, or 5.30 Pacific time, so I have to wait for the dining car to open. I sip my coffee through the plastic lid and listen to Toni talking to herself across the corridor. I generally hate plastic lids on drinks, but on a train it does make some sense.

Breakfast always looks better in the sunshine. This morning the baking sun disguises the low temperature outside. It streams into the opposite side of the dining car to where I'm seated with some passengers who have spent the night in coach class. The routine is always the same. An upside-down paper coffee cup acts as a holder for a few stubby little pens. The attendant asks you to write your name and room number on a form and sign and date it. I order an omelette with sausage and breakfast potatoes and Cheddar cheese, to be a bit different, but I doubt it comes from Cheddar. Amtrak sausage is well spiced and a much better choice than the bacon. Seated opposite me are Atsa, a Navajo Indian doctor and his daughter Ooljee, who is a medical student. They are absolutely charming people and once again I'm thankful for the railroad tradition of community seating. I would love to spend more time with them. When I think of the Navajo it's their amazing code talkers from the Second World War that first come to mind. But I know nothing of their history, culture and spiritual beliefs. Ooljee suggests I spend some time in Santa Fe to learn more. Atsa works in a hospital as a consultant specialising in infectious diseases. He tells me he's worried about a new deadly virus that is going around in the north-eastern United States at the moment and that I should be really careful when I head back to Chicago. When I tell them that I'm getting off at Albuquerque today they seem quite pleased. They are interested on what I'm planning to do when I get there, as it's not a tourist town.

The train is running on time this morning. The Chief is scheduled to take around 45 hours to cover the distance to Chicago, and I can imagine that a long delay would be a real pain. The poster I saw in the lounge in LA said it was 39 hours, but the route has changed over time. This train is one of the fastest running Amtrak long-distance services. The train can operate at speeds of up to 90 mph in places, because those sections of the line have an automatic train-stop system installed. This is a legacy of the Atchison, Topeka and Santa Fe Railway. But the problem lies between Lamy, New Mexico, and La Junta in Colorado. Here the line here is not used by freight, and Amtrak has to pay to maintain it. It's not only much slower here, but also the maintenance is something that Amtrak can ill afford. A couple of years ago it was proposed that a replacement bus service would run between Albuquerque and Dodge City, but this was averted with federal grants. It would be an incredibly sad day if the route of the Chief were literally cut in two.

When Toni comes to check that I know I'm getting off at the next stop I'm already pretty much packed. She is going all the way to Chicago and then back to LA, working four days on then five days off. She prefers the Chief to the Sunset Limited as the Chief's schedule is normally more reliable.

The engineer calls the stop a few minutes before we arrive, so I do some final checks that I haven't left anything behind and head downstairs to wait. The train stops here for half an hour to refuel, so it's unlikely that I'm going to fail to get off in time, but this is one of the few trips where I'm not travelling on to the final destination. In the lower lobby of the carriage I find I'm the only passenger leaving the train here at Albuquerque. I'm also surprised to find Atsa and Ooljee waiting for me. They have walked all the way down from their coach carriage to see me off. I'm taken back by such an act of friendship towards someone they only met four hours ago. I try to shake Asta's hand but he stops me and instead we do elbow bumps. It's the best way to stay safe, he tells me. I must find out more about this virus. Once I'm down on the platform I say farewell to Toni and wave at my Navajo friends, who are now standing just inside the open carriage door. 'Bye bye, Matthew,' says Ooljee, and with a tear in my eye I have to turn my back and cross the tracks to reach the station building.

Chapter Eleven
Better Call Salzar

Albuquerque station is actually called the Alvarado Transportation Center. It's a nice enough place, low-rise buildings with plenty of shade from the sun, and a pretty clock tower. The design style is called Mission Revival, and the look came from a hotel of the same name that used to be here. Reunited with my bag, I stroll around looking for a taxi but there are none, so it's the usual drill: go to the ticket office and ask them nicely if they can call me one. 'Look out for a white car,' the really friendly lady says. 'It'll have a Z on it.'

I'm quite happy standing outside in the sunshine, warming my body and lifting my spirit. The Z-Trip taxi driver cruises by and spots me before I see him. With the bags on board we set off to a corner of town known for cheap hotels and freeway overpasses rather than culture or nightlife. On the radio soothing music is interspersed

183

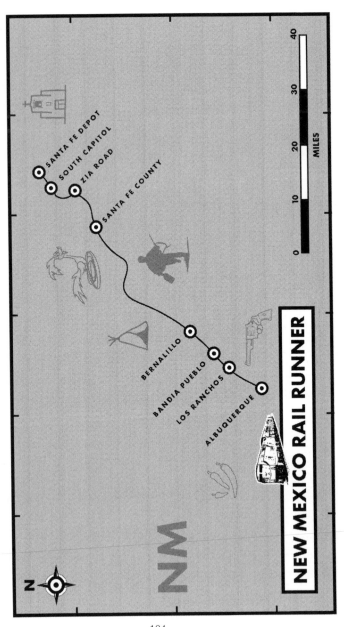

SANTA FE DEPOT
SOUTH CAPITOL
ZIA ROAD
SANTA FE COUNTY
BERNALILLO
BANDIA PUEBLO
LOS RANCHOS
ALBUQUERQUE

N

NM

NEW MEXICO RAIL RUNNER

MILES

0   10   20   30   40

with cheesy adverts for retirement homes and Mexican restaurant happy hours. He tells me he's an out-of-work actor bound for a new life in New Zealand in a couple of months' time, and he wants to know why I'm here. Dropping me off outside my nondescript hotel he shakes my hand and gives me his business card. He's handwritten a message on one side. Along with his private cell number, it says simply 'Better Call Salzar'.

My drab-looking hotel turns out to be pleasant enough inside. There is even a little waterfall in reception, where the staff are used to dealing with travelling sales reps and delegates from conferences who can't afford to stay at the main venue in town. There is an outdoor pool, but it's closed as this is the middle of winter. Strange, as to me it feels like summer. Most importantly, though, it has a nice little bar and a restaurant that serves an all-American breakfast. When I open the door to my room I'm transported back to the 1980s. Chintzy fabrics, patterned and peeling wallpaper, and beaten-up furniture. Pulling back the net curtains I'm greeted with a direct view out over an elevated junction of the freeway. But I'm in such a good mood that I don't care. I'm not going to spend any time here, and when you've been living in an Amtrak roomette, any hotel room is large and exciting. Plus you get an ensuite bathroom, your own coffee maker and even a television.

I'm finding that even rather dull hotels in the United States can have quite good bars. It's also quite normal to find a good range of draught beers and also to be able to eat a reasonable meal whilst sat at the bar. In the early evening I have a couple of beers and a chat with those around me at the bar. To my right sits Tony, a larger-than-life man from Brooklyn, together with his slightly embarrassed wife. Tony wants to know what I'm up to. He's amazed I've made it all the way from his home around the States to Albuquerque by rail. His wife looks up Amtrak on her phone, as if unsure that it's even possible, but once she's suitably convinced the conversation continues. She's a psychiatrist, he's a professional gambler. I had Tony down to be in the waste disposal business, like his namesake, Tony Soprano. But it's almost as good, as he's a larger-than-life chap.

At the other end of the bar is Kyle, an engineer from NASA in Houston. Small world. He's working on a problem out at Kirkland air force base. Nothing too tricky he tells me, but I have a suspicion that nonetheless, it *is* rocket science. Kyle is keen to get my views on European politics. I've noticed that Americans seem quite relaxed talking politics, something that might be bad form in the pub back home.

It's quite good fun here, but I'm not going to spend my evening in the hotel. The bartender suggests a few local places where I can eat, so wishing everyone well I wander out into the darkness. It's probably not a good part of town, so I keep moving and stay close to the streetlights.

On my little map everything looks close by, but in fact it's miles away. The place I'm looking for is called Little Anita's. It's nothing special, but well known for all the local dishes that I want to try. Once I have got to grips with the scale of the map, I find Little Anita's where it's supposed to be, surrounded by hardware shops and liquor stores. The manager offers me a table by the window, but I choose to sit at the counter where I can watch the chefs prepare the food that's leaving the busy kitchen. It's a bit sticky and grimy back there, but I try not to let that put me off – after all, the chilis will protect me from any bacteria.

The menu is enormous and I need the help of the server to help me order. Tostadas, carnitas, enchiladas and tacos dominate what's on offer. Green chilis are pretty much mandatory, and you're never far from a bowl of nachos. I opt for some fish tacos followed by tamales, a kind of dough pancake stuffed with chilis and cheese. Unfamiliar with New Mexican cuisine, as I am, this is educational. Whilst I wait for my food I ask the chef to identify the dishes leaving the kitchen. It's challenging, as many of the plates are drowning in a gloopy-looking chili sauce. But when I look up at the reception desk by the door I completely forget about the food. A man who appears quite out of place here has arrived. He looks to be in his 50s and he sports round metal-framed glasses and a smart suit. He has dark skin and short hair. Straightening his tie, he smiles nicely at the receptionist and spots me staring at him before I can look away. I'm sure I have seen him before – this can't be a coincidence. Someone has worked really hard basing their image on the infamous Gustavo Fring from *Breaking Bad*, a highly regarded television series filmed in Albuquerque.

Completely stuffed with cheese and lips tingling from all the chilis, I ask for the bill. It's taken me a while to get used to properly tipping. Being British I'm not used to adding so much money to the bill. But it's a really big deal here in the States, where the taxman assumes the level of tip, and taxes service staff accordingly as part of their earnings. Although food has been included with my ticket on board the trains, I have still been leaving a tip, but I have noticed that not everyone does. I don't want to be remembered as the tight-fisted Englishman, and I'm really grateful to be welcomed and looked after everywhere, so I try and leave at least 20 per cent. A 10 per cent tip here is code for 'the service was awful'. I buy into the unwritten contract between the staff and customer. The staff assume you will tip them and work extra hard to make your experience as good as it can be. They rely on this as they are often poorly paid. Rather than behaving like underpaid staff, they smile, they listen to your stories however boring they might be, and they look after you.

The walk back to the hotel in the cool evening air allows my stomach to settle. With the curtains open in my room I have a view of the traffic on the freeway, the headlights whizzing past in a hypnotic procession. I'm very content here. Staying in a cheap business hotel highlights the enjoyment I derive from everyday American life. I don't know how long I stare at the freeway for before I fall asleep on the bed fully clothed.

The following morning Salzar drops me off at the railroad station. I'm not leaving Albuquerque just yet, but heading to Santa Fe on a day trip. The station isn't only home to Amtrak, but also to a state-run train, the New Mexico Rail Runner, which connects the two cities. To begin with I'm alone on the platform. It's much colder than I'd expected. Shorts might not have been the right choice, but the sun is slowly rising and I'm hopeful that it will warm me through. The Rail Runner operates on a different line from that of the Amtrak services that pass through Albuquerque, but the platform is close by. I find a shelter and sit down to wait for my train to arrive. I might not have brought a jumper, but I didn't forget breakfast. I fish out a paper bag that is warm in my hands and smells good. Inside, is a breakfast burrito, a fat tortilla filled with eggs, bacon, chilis and cheese, and it tastes heavenly. The waitress in Little Anita's had asked me if I wanted the Christmas version, which is made out of both red and green chilis like a Christmas tree. How could I refuse?

A few other passengers begin to arrive, but no one looks like they are in a hurry. Before too long the Rail Runner pulls in on the platform right in front of me. It's a cool-looking train. The locomotive is silver, aerodynamic and painted with the roadrunner bird on its sides. Beneath the windows of the cab is a single light and the wings of a bird painted in red and orange. On the sides of the locomotive, behind the cab, is a painting of the head of the bird. Above the train's number the words 'Rail Runner Express' are printed in a stylish font. It pulls three or four duplex carriages behind it with a matching paint scheme, and a second locomotive is attached at the other end in a permanent push–pull configuration. If you are a rail fan you will know these are MP36PH-3C locomotives, built by a company called MotivePower. They are the only locomotives on sale in the United States at the moment, as no other train meets the new Tier 4 emission standards. If you are of a certain age you might remember that the roadrunner was a cartoon character in a cartoon made by Warner Brothers, alongside Bugs Bunny, under the *Looney Tunes* banner. The plot is simple. In every episode Wile E. Coyote tries to catch and eat the roadrunner using all sorts of strange devices, most mailed to him from a company called ACME. But since 1949 the roadrunner, or chaparral bird, has also been the state bird of New Mexico. Whoever does the marketing for Rio Metro, the train operating company, has done an amazing job.

The driver climbs down from the cab and leaves the train with the doors open for passengers to get on, half an hour until we are due to depart. None of the British shenanigans of not announcing the platform until the last minute, or locking the doors until 5 minutes before departure, here. I've even got time to take some photographs of this exotic-looking train. With this task complete and nothing else of interest on the platform, I climb aboard. I have no seat reservation. In fact, I have no ticket either. I have been told it's easier to buy a ticket once we are under way. This is a blessing, but also a problem for me. Where am I going to sit? In an almost empty carriage I have far too many choices. Lower deck, mezzanine mid-level, or upper deck? Window or aisle? Twin seats, or four with a table? I try to work out where the sun might eventually be and try a few places out. The seats are both jazzy-looking and very comfortable. I'm conditioned to prefer sitting up top, and claim what I think is the best seat in the carriage. Passengers start to drift in and find their preferred seats all around me.

A well-tanned man wearing hiking gear emerges at the top of the stairs to the upper deck. He says 'Howdy' to me. Do I mind if he sits here? he asks me. 'No problemo,' I reply, gesturing him to the free seat opposite. No one has ever said 'Howdy' to me before, and without thinking my reply was straight out of *Terminator 2*. It's a phrase John Connor teaches the Model 101 Terminator to use in order to blend in, along with the perhaps more memorable phrase 'Hasta la vista, baby.' Ron introduces himself. He's a retired American teacher walking across various parts of the world. He's even going to walk across Wales in a few months' time, and he's keen to discover if all the things he has heard about the Welsh are true. We discuss the climate, Tom Jones, rugby and strange vegetables until I run out of decisive facts, which doesn't take long at all.

The Rail Runner came into service in 2006, creating a commuter service serving the corridor between Belen and Santa Fe. It has 97 miles of line serving sixteen stations, and eleven trains run each day in both directions. Costing $365 million to build, it was designed to take commuter and tourism traffic off the road, but passenger numbers have now been falling for over a decade. People blame the low price of oil, encouraging road transport, and the lack of frequent trains. This seems rather a shame as it's a train I'd love to commute on, but I see the problem. Today there are five morning services running to Santa Fe. I've had to choose between 04.32, 05.02, 06.22, 07.19 and 09.35. Needless to say, I'm on the last of these.

The engineer says hello on the PA before we set off, and runs through the stops ahead. The names of the Native American settlements en route sound unusual to my ear and interesting – Montaño, Sandia Pueblo, Bernalillo and Kewa. But the best bit about our departure has been saved until last. The doors don't just close with a warning tone. They close with a 'meep meep' jingle, the call of the cartoon roadrunner bird. Bob and I can't help but smile at each other when this happens. It really is a cool train.

The ticket attendant works her way down the coach chatting to her passengers and answering questions whilst printing out tickets with a big portable machine. I seem to be the only person not getting some sort of discount today. I part with a crisp $20 note, my return fare. Outside the scenery is mixed, but out of the towns it is characterised by the nothingness of desert with the occasional pueblos of the Native Americans. New Mexico has 23 tribes, each with its own government, jurisdiction and laws. No one mentions it to me on the train, but I have read that it's bad form to take photos of these reservations, so I leave my camera in the bag and just enjoy the journey. I think of my friends Atsa and Ooljee, and wonder if they live in one of these indigenous towns built of stone and mud.

I'm also thinking about films again. This the landscape of the Coen brothers' 2007 movie, *No Country for Old Men*, a dark and at times violent thriller based closely on Cormac McCarthy's book of the same name. Production took place in Albuquerque, Santa Fe and Las Vegas (the Las Vegas in New Mexico; I have found out that there are two places with the same name). Perhaps one of their finest films, it was nominated for eight Oscars. Surely no one will ever forget Javier Bardem, who won an Oscar for his performance as best actor in a supporting role. He was also the first Spanish actor ever to win an Oscar. I'm not a fan of Tommy Lee Jones, and I doubt Joel and Ethan Coen are either. Tommy sued Paramount for improper expense reductions and eventually received a settlement of $17 million.

Looking at my Cannonball as we pull into the railyard at Santa Fe, I see we have arrived on time at 11.16, and with a 'meep, meep' I'm safely down on the platform with no coyotes in sight. It was cold in Albuquerque, but a further 500 metres higher in Santa Fe it's absolutely freezing. Bugger. I need to buy time, so I find a coffee shop nearby and consider my options. Luckily for me, I have stumbled upon Sky Coffee, the friendliest coffee shop in these parts. It's one of those places where people come to hang out, and the coffee is weapons grade. Santa Fe has a big arts scene and is seen as a desirable place for people who want to escape big cities to come to live, and coffee culture is enshrined in the culture. They have time to chat, and they like the good things in life. A chap at the next table shuts his MacBook and introduces himself as Brad. He orientates my map and suggests a few places to visit. When I look up from the map the whole café are listening in, and several offer their advice. They all laugh when I explain my sartorial error with the shorts and shirt, but they're not laughing at me, more with me. Brad even offers me the loan of a jacket for the day, and I accept. Once again I'm bowled over by the friendliness and helpfulness of everyday Americans.

I imagine that Santa Fe railyard is a brilliant place to hang out in the summer with its farmers market, artisan stalls and bars and restaurants. But today on a winter weekday it's bloody cold and there's nothing happening outside so I set off at a brisk pace in the direction of the old town. The architecture everywhere is the same style, with flat roofs, and protruding beams and porchways. They call it Spanish Territorial.

I have to keep moving, as even with Brad's trendy and too-small-to-zip-up jacket on, my bare legs have become chicken-like. Finding my bearings, I head down South Guadalupe Street, where I find the central plaza and some of the city's more famous landmarks. Salzar has told me about the Loretto Chapel, so when I find it I step inside the doors to see the miracle for myself. Built in the 1880s, it had been designed by a Frenchman called Antoine Mouly, who died before the building was finished. The nuns prayed to St Joseph, the patron saint of carpenters, for a solution to their problem – they had no way of getting up into the choir loft. The chapel was too small for a staircase, and their attire would not suit a ladder. Out of the blue a workman turned up one day and offered to build them a staircase, but he insisted that it had to be done in private. The nuns agreed and a wooden spiral staircase was built. The staircase has nothing visibly supporting it, and uses no nails or glue, just wooden pegs to hold it together. They call it St Joseph's Staircase.

Predictably for me, I'm fast reaching cultural overload. In Asia they call it being 'templed out'. I'm cold, and my mind is distracted from the Sisters of Loretto by naughty thoughts. Try not to hold this against me. I have the feeling of being on a school field trip with the possibility of bunking off without being spotted. I carefully look over each shoulder, but no one's paying attention to me, just the spiral staircase. So I casually retrace my steps back out onto the chilly street. I have a plan. It isn't particularly cunning, but I like the broad brushstrokes. It involves beer, food and warmth. It doesn't take long to find a place not too far away called The Cowgirl. The sign outside, not unsurprisingly, is of a dancing cowgirl next to a plaque that reads 'BBQ & Smokehouse'. Perfect.

The bar is full of men sitting on stools wearing chaps, trendy waistcoats and cowboy hats. If you have seen *The Blues Brothers*, this would be the sort of place that the Good Ol' Boys would have a drink in before going on stage. Some of them look up and study the man with a hiking jacket, shorts and sandals. I don't have long to decide what to do, but with growing confidence in my Americanisms, I say 'Howdy' as loudly as I dare. A couple of them smile at me, and the rest return to their conversations about the price of hogs and the latest lasso techniques. Without fuss I'm shown to a table with a red and white checked cloth and a huge range of condiments, mainly hot sauces. Now I really wish I that I had purchased my own cowboy hat when I was in Houston.

The server, dressed as a cowgirl, pops by and leaves an impressive beer list for me to study together with a menu – more specifically a BBQ'd dead animal and chili menu. From the dozens of draft beers I elect to try a tasting selection of Sierra Nevada beers, a wooden tray with glasses of IPA, Freestyle Pilsner, Hazy Lil' Thing and Oktoberfest. The burger I choose is called 'The Mother of all Green Chili Cheeseburgers', but my friendly cowgirl tells me that I can just refer to it as 'The Mother'. It doesn't disappoint, but my heart surgeon might have a different opinion. The combination of alcohol and chili gives me an instant high, warming my heart and soul. I could spend most of the day here, but glancing at my Cannonball, it's only 10 minutes until the next Rail Runner is heading back to Albuquerque. I feel guilty for not spending longer in the city and vow to return – in the summer.

I am about to get on the train when I have a nagging doubt that something's not quite right. I check that I have my bag, my notebook, my wallet and watch. All present and correct. Then I remember – I've still got Brad's jacket. I set off at a jog back to the Sky coffee shop, reminding myself that I really don't enjoy jogging. Behind me I hear the 'meep meep' of the doors of the Rail Runner opening. Inside Brad is nowhere to be seen, so I hand it to someone I recognise. I don't have time to say thank you properly, so I hold my thumbs aloft as I gasp for air, turn and run for the train, which I make with 30 seconds to spare. With a final 'meep meep' and a blast of the horn we begin the return journey to Albuquerque.

Back at my hotel bar nothing much has changed in the few hours I've been away. When I walk through the bar Tony spots me and declares 'Hey, here's the rail guy.' I quite enjoy the minor notoriety and pull up my usual seat for a quick chat. A bar where everybody knows your name. Wasn't that the theme song to *Cheers* in the 1980s? I love American bars. I could get used to this, but my stomach is now dealing with trying to process more high-end chili eaten in the last two days than the average European eats in two years. My body provides little warning of the impending result of this, but I make it to the restroom just in time, and recite a well-known Elvis Presley song until it's all over. I spend the rest of the evening in the comfort of my own ensuite bathroom and feel a lot better a couple of hours later. It's an early night tonight, as I will have to have my wits about me for tomorrow's induction into the right to bear arms.

Chapter Twelve
Dirty Matthew

The following lunchtime Salzar drops me off outside the gun store and tells me to call him if I need any help. I'm not sure what he means by that, but I now have his number saved as a speed dial on my phone. I wave it at him as he smiles knowingly and drives off across the empty parking lot. I had decided that in order to better understand life in America and the American obsession with firearms, I needed to visit a gun store. I was in luck, as I discovered Albuquerque has many such shops. They even have shooting ranges where you can try out your favourite lethal weapons before buying them. New Mexico has a strong gun culture, and no licence is required to buy and own most guns, as long as you don't have a criminal record. Let me say that again – absolutely no licence is required. That is almost unbelievable to someone from the United Kingdom, a country where the policeman are mostly unarmed, and for you to own anything more powerful than an airgun you must obtain a licence – which is only issued, if at all, after checking with your doctor and a police visit to your home to check on your security arrangements. Here in New Mexico, if you're prepared to allow background checks and complete a short safety course, you are issued a permit that allows you to carry a concealed loaded firearm in a public place.

I do my best to forget about these incredibly liberal laws and the statistics which show Albuquerque to be one of the most dangerous cities in the United States. No time to change my mind now, I tell myself, as I push open the mirrored glass doors of the fairly anonymous-looking industrial unit. Inside, the atmosphere is calm, and the air conditioning is set to frosty. The lady behind reception doesn't know about my specially arranged visit, but says she'll go and fetch Mike. As I wait by the counter for Mike I decide to have a look around. Am I allowed to do that? I do my best at looking casual. The nearest wall to me is covered in rifles. Not the sort you hunt with, but the sort you defend yourself from the apocalypse with. Unsure of gun shop etiquette, I don't touch any of them but instead wander up and down as if I'm inspecting a parade. Still no Mike, so I make bigger and bigger circuits of the store. In the middle is an area with glass cases packed with handguns and a couple of members of staff showing various models to customers. One of them looks up and asks if I need help. I tell him I'm waiting for Mike. It turns out he's called Mike too, as is the other man behind the counter.

When the right Mike returns from his break he looks in his book and finds my name. 'Ah, Matt – you're all in,' he tells me. 'All in?' I ask. 'You're going to have real fun; we have you booked in to shoot everything we got. Only problem is the firing pin on the Galil is broken, but I think I can fix it.' I have never seen a Galil before, but I'm pretty sure it's one of those ingenious Israeli weapons – one that even has a wire cutter and a bottle opener set into the carrying handle – not that a beer is on the cards here.

Before I can tell Mike that the Galil isn't a dealbreaker to our arrangement, he catches the attention of the other Mikes and tells them I'm 'all in', which causes a flurry of activity from the other side of the counter. They begin to stack boxes of ammunition on the glass top and find magazines of assorted sizes. I try not to let my nervousness show as bigger and still bigger bullets are added to the pile, but at least there is time to chat as two of the three Mikes load rounds into the magazines. The third Mike has found a hospital trolley and begun to stack an assortment of firearms onto it.

When I was in LA I ran out of time to follow up on the locations of several key films shot on location in the city. *Terminator 2* had been partly filmed in Santa Monica, but it was the first movie in the Terminator franchise that was on my mind. Released in 1984, a Cyberdine Systems

Model 101 travels back in time from a future world, arriving in a parking lot in downtown LA. The rest is history. It made the careers of its director, James Cameron, and its leading actor, Arnold Schwarzenegger. The film is pretty basic, but back then it helped define a whole new genre of gritty chilling sci-fi touching our own world.

There is one scene that I will always remember, where the Terminator visits Alamo Guns, a local sports shop at Van Nuys in the San Fernando valley. He needs to equip himself to eliminate Sarah Connor, the mother of the future leader of the resistance movement. Inside he talks to Rob Garrett, the owner of the gun store, who offers him various weapons on display. Arnie tries out a 12-gauge autoloader (pump action shotgun), a .45 long slide with laser sighting (huge pistol) and a Uzi 9mm (submachine gun). He also asks Rob for a 'phased plasma rifle in the 40-watt range', but Rob replies, 'Hey, just what you see, pal.' There is something unforgettable and chilling about hearing the words 'Uzi 9-millimeter' spoken with a heavy Austrian accent. Rather sadly, Rob's time on screen before the Terminator terminates him is less than one minute and today the gun store in the film is a car dealership.

Back in this gun store I can see the autoloaders, the long slides and even the Uzi. They are on the back counter behind the growing pile of ammunition. The first Mike asks me if I have shot any of these before. I tell him no, but that I used to shoot a Lee Enfield .303 when I was a small soldier, which seems to impress him. 'What do you want to shoot first?' he asks. I think about this for a moment, peering at the pile of weapons on test. There is a growing schoolboy urge to ask for the Uzi in the style of Arnold Schwarzenegger. Despite pinching myself and doing all I can to resist the temptation, I just can't stop myself, only just managing to avoid doing so with an Austrian accent. 'Can I try the Uzi 9 millimeter, please?' It comes out as though I'm ordering a glass of wine in a nice restaurant. Mike thinks that's a good choice and nods approvingly, but the other Mikes haven't loaded any 9mm Parabellum rounds into suitable magazines yet. Instead he makes a quick decision that he's going to throw me in at the deep end. 'You wanna try this one first?' he says, pushing a simply enormous nickel-plated pistol across the counter in my direction. 'It's a Smith & Wesson .50 cal – the biggest, most powerful revolver in the whole world.' I try to pick it up, but it's way heavier than I have assumed, so I try again with both hands. Leaving the stack of guns on the trolley, he hands me some ear defenders and shows me out through some security doors to the range next door. You can't open the second door until the first door is closed. I'm not sure if this is for noise protection or to keep a madman with live weapons out of the store in an emergency.

The range is large and dimly lit, just the whir of air conditioning, and otherwise all is quiet. Spotlights shine on the target area of the range. The walls are painted black, and you can't really see them. There are maybe a dozen lanes, each equipped with a screened-off firing point and a bench table to stack ammunition on. From my little partitioned booth Mike finds a full-size target of a man running towards me with an expression of extreme prejudice, and clips it onto the rail overhead. He holds the button on the wall down and the target speeds off down the range. How far back is it going? Anyone who has seen *Lethal Weapon* will remember Danny Glover playing Roger Murtaugh with his Smith & Wesson 19 and Mel Gibson as Martin Riggs with a Beretta 92F. It's actually the same replica gun that Bruce Willis used in the making of *Die Hard* the following year. Anyway, Glover goes first, and on inspection of the target says proudly 'not bad for an old man' to Gibson. Mel then pushes his target back so far that you can't see it, offloads the 15 rounds in the Beretta and brings the target back in. The holes in the target form a smiley face with both eyes and a nose. 'Have a nice day,' he says before walking off.

Mike sets the target about halfway down the range, maybe 10 metres away, and proceeds to load the gun for me. He pops the bullets in one by one then snaps the cylinder shut and spins it, I assume for theatrical effect, before passing it over to me. Holding it in both my hands requires some effort, not just because of its weight, but its sheer size. You might recognise the proportions from the film *Dirty Harry*, except that this one is even bigger.

Clint Eastwood's Harry Callahan used a .44 Magnum produced by the same manufacturer. Hoping Mike won't laugh, I adopt a squatting stance familiar to anyone who was a fan of the television show *The Professionals*. I hang onto the oversized rubberised grips, focus the foresight of the 10.5-inch barrel on the centre of the target and pull the trigger gently. The hammer comes back towards me before smashing the firing pin into the back of the shell in the chamber. A moment of quiet calm, then the barrel leaps up in the air and the energy of the .50 bullet pushes me backwards. It's quite outrageous, and the only reason I could see for owning such a weapon would be for close protection from large dinosaurs. Repeating the process a few times, I eventually hold the barrel down enough to hit the target. Then on my sixth shot the hammer goes forward but there is just a big click and a comedy movement as I pull downwards with my arms a fraction of a second later when nothing happens. The bullets are so big only five fit in the revolver, rather than the six in Clint's magnum.

Over the next couple of hours a carpet of empty brass shells forms on the concrete floor of my firing point. The Mikes bring in trolley loads of weapons and take it in turns to look after me. In my head I simulate gun battles in the jungles of South East Asia, urban warfare in the Middle East and fighting through wadis in Afghanistan, using the appropriate weapons from each conflict.

The final rifle that Mike brings in to me is too big to fit

on a trolley. He carefully carries it in and rests it on a chair – it's too heavy to hold. 'Here's the beast,' he tells me. 'You get just one shot – it's all you'll need.' The weapon is an Armalite AR-50, a single shot rifle. But that single shot is all that's needed. Its BMG bullet is the most powerful rifle round in the world, capable of shooting through walls at a range of over 2000 yards. If you ever saw the television show *Better Call Saul*, which was filmed in the city, this is rifle that Mike Ehrmantraut is offered to use for the contract killing of Tuco Salamanca, a local cartel drug dealer. Ehrmantraut looks at the gun in the motel bedroom and tells his arms dealer, 'It looks like a hernia with a scope on it ... too much gun.'

I can sense a certain anticipation, or even tension, building from Mike's expression. He pulls up a plastic chair and sets the rifle up with its bipod on the table in front of me. Once I'm comfortable holding it he helps me chamber a bullet that I find is longer than my hand when I pick it up. Apparently, I'm good to go once he taps me on the shoulder twice. First of all, though, he shouts, 'Fire in the hole!' to warn other shooters to hang on before he gives me the signal. It's over to me now to complete the mission. The trigger is smooth and easy, after all this is a sniper's rifle, but when the round goes off inside the 50-inch barrel, all hell breaks loose. From my position I can see the flash and flames that follow the bullet out of the barrel, and then the deafening noise of the explosion just inches from my head. The rifle weighs over 34 pounds, which holds it down on the ground, but

I feel a mule has just kicked me in my right shoulder. I manage to keep my eyes on the target through the telescopic sight. It doesn't just get a hole in it; the energy of the bullet lifts the whole target in the air as the bullet passes through it. On the imaginary radio set in my head: 'Bravo, Matthew Zero, mission accomplished. Return to base.'

Back in the store I have a new-found swagger. I'm briefly the star of the show, the punter who has biggest brag. The man who fired the AR-50 and lived to tell the tale. I can't resist suggesting to the man next to me who is inspecting a selection of Glock 17s that he considers something bigger. Call that a gun? Ha, it's a water pistol.

I thank the three Mikes for keeping me safe and ask the receptionist to call Salzar, as I can't get seem to get through to him on my phone. Sitting alone on a concrete bench outside the store in the late afternoon sun, I'm in a reflective mood. It's quiet here, just the sound of distant traffic on the freeway. You can't hear the gunfire from the range.

The adrenaline rush I'm feeling troubles me. These guns are not designed for hunting or even home defence - they're for fighting wars and killing people. In the United States there are an estimated 120 guns per 100 people. No surprise that more than 70 per cent of homicides are gun-related. There is a new law on the table where the police can take guns away from people, but I hear locally that they don't want that power.

One side of my brain is hard-wired to enjoy shooting and playing with guns. I grew up with toy guns, playing cowboys and reading magazines called *Warlord* and *Commando*. The other side of my head is thankful that we don't have guns like this in my world at home. Okay we have occasional violent crime, we have knife crime – but surely the sort of thing I'm seeing here would ruin our society. Or will the people I meet here tell me that it's nothing to do with the gun, but the person who pulls the trigger? Will they say that if it's not a gun then it's a knife, so it makes no real difference? I'm going to have to tread carefully, finding out what Americans think about this. It's very clear that shooting is portrayed as serious fun by the pro-gun lobby – bring the family along, shoot some things on the range, have a BBQ. It's an embedded part of living the dream.

Salzar honks his horn. I'm lost in my thoughts. On the way back to my hotel we talk about the need to carry a gun. He tells me he carries .38 in his glove box, no permit required. When he lived in Alaska the police told him off for not having a bigger calibre gun – apparently a .38 isn't good enough for defence from wild bears in the woods. I tell him I know just the revolver for him, if he's willing to work out a bit more in the gym.

One tip Mike has given me is to wash with soap and cold water, as hot water will let the gunshot residue covering my body sink into the pores of my skin. So it's a long scrub in a cold shower before I head to the bar where I can slowly come down with a couple of beers and chat about the football game on the big screen. There is a game that I have started to play with myself: can I pretend to know enough about the sport to convince the person sitting next to me that I am a fan of the team I'm pretending to support? It's a confidence builder, as you have to be fully committed to getting away with it. I have a secret weapon, though, in the form of my friend and NFL advisor James Devlin in Chicago. We swap texts and he feeds me all the player facts and the killer lines to drop into casual football banter. All seems to be going well this evening, and I throw in a few screams of outrage and a couple of cheers, hopefully at the right moments. I'm trying to work towards actually supporting an NFL team, but can't work out which one it should be.

On my final day in Albuquerque I have planned something a bit special. I've been given a rendezvous location to meet a man called Mitch behind a church in the old town. Salzar can't find the spot at first, but skirting round the plaza he eventually works it out and leaves me in a nondescript back street where all is quiet. It's early, and it's one of those almost guaranteed New Mexico mornings of saturated blue sky and the sun slowly rising above the distant mountains to heat everything up. I haven't seen a cloud since I arrived. There are a few other people hanging around here, and I suspect they're here for the same reason as me, to hook up with Mitch. I cautiously ask a couple if they know him. They say they don't, but like me they are keen to meet him.

We hear Mitch before we see him driving our transport for the day: the very distinctive rumble of the big block Chevvy engine powering the Fleetwood Bounder motorhome as it passes behind the low-rise buildings. When he turns the corner into our street the whole vehicle leans over alarmingly to one side as the suspension fails to cope with his enthusiastic driving style. Back on the straight, the body of the battered motorhome settles back upright and he comes to a halt in front of us. 'Morning!' he shouts out the front window from behind some cool shades, before adding, 'Let's bounce!'

Breaking Bad first came to the UK's television screens in January 2008. It was the story of Walter White, a chemistry teacher with cancer turning to a life of crime to look after his family. Five years and 62 episodes later, it had become the most critically acclaimed show ever made. It was set entirely in Albuquerque, and its creator, Vince Gilligan, had been drawn to the city by the tax credits available to film makers in New Mexico, but rather than hide the location of his series he made its locations a feature of the plot. Walter White and his partner in crime, Jesse Pinkman, set up a crystal methamphetamine lab in a Fleetwood Bounder in the first few episodes, and as a result the vehicle has iconic status amongst fans of the show.

It's immediately obvious that not only is Mitch is quite cool, he's also a really nice guy. He checks each of us in, apologising for a slight delay in starting as his partner Luigi has to 'clean things up a bit from yesterday's show', whatever that means. Once this is done he ushers us up the steps and into the Bounder. Climbing the step I can't help noticing the detail, right down to some bullet holes in the door. I wondered what it might look like inside, and the answer is just like it does on television but with a half a dozen seats added. I find one at the back, behind a plastic drum of phenylacetic acid and some complex-looking meth-cooking glassware. How will all of this stuff will stay in one piece when we go around corners, I wonder. I'm not one of the world's great smilers, but I find myself with a grin like a Cheshire cat – this is incredible: a deep dive into the world of *Breaking Bad*. But it gets even better. Not only is Mitch an expert on the series – he even had a part as a DEA agent in one season of the show.

The health and safety briefing is straightforward: sit down when he or Luigi rings the bell on the dashboard. But just as importantly, before we can leave he makes us practise a few Jesse Pinkman phrases to ensure we're good enough for the road. Most involve the words 'yo!', 'okay, bitch!' and 'what's up?' Warm-up complete, he rings the bell and declares, 'We're rolling!' as we sway down the road towards our first destination. The people on the street seem to ignore us – five years of location filming have obviously taken their toll. This is the new normal for downtown Albuquerque.

As we cruise around town Mitch points out locations from all sorts of films before we stop at Twisters, a budget chain chicken restaurant on the edge of town. Except of course, to any of the ten million viewers of *Breaking Bad* it's not Twisters. This is Los Pollos Hermanos, the cover for Gus Fring's narcotic smuggling and distribution empire – the man I thought I saw in Little Anita's just the other day. Then on to Walt's house, the Doghouse, and the car wash. All are totally familiar, but yet so strange when you actually visit them. We also stop at the laundry where Gus builds Walt and Jesse's state-of-the-art meth superlab. Not only is at a real laundry, but some of the workers we meet, mainly Mexican ladies, actually appeared in the show. Here the boundaries of fictional television and everyday Albuquerque reality are blurred.

One episode of *Breaking Bad* featured a railway hijack. Season 5, Episode 5 (why do they call it a season, when it always used to be a series?) is titled 'Dead Freight'. The tracks south of Santa Fe, at a place called Lamy, are the setting for the elaborate theft of bulk methylamine from a train. By coincidence the very same stretch of track with the same bridge was used for some of the train sequences in *Butch Cassidy and the Sundance Kid* forty-four years earlier. I will be passing through Lamy on the Southwest Chief tomorrow, and I wonder if I will spot it.

In 2019 a sequel was released as a film, called *El Camino*. It follows Jesse Pinkman in the aftermath of *Breaking Bad*. As it was filmed under a veil of secrecy, hardly anyone knew it existed until production had finished. Mitch explains that the Bounder we are in today was used in the diner sequence in the film, shot at the Owl Café. The cover story they used was that they were filming a commercial for a *Breaking Bad* RV tour. Bryan Cranston was smuggled in from LA on a private jet in heavy disguise. Everyone in the diner was vetted and sworn to secrecy. This was a clever and highly plausible cover story, given that it's exactly what we're up to today.

Mitch and I have a quick chat at the car wash, where he asks me what I'm up to at the weekend. It's the premier of the new season of the prequel show, *Better Call Saul*, and they're having a party to celebrate. He says he wants to introduce me to his friend Gonzo, Tuco Sulamanca's brother-in-law in the show. Whilst I'd love to hang out with them, I explain that have to catch the Chief tomorrow (or in my mind the Silver Streak). I tell him to pass my best on to his cartel friends, and I say that I hope to return.

Silver Streak

Chapter Thirteen
The Mighty Chief

Albuquerque station is quiet and peaceful today, and check-in only takes a couple of minutes. Finding a bench to sit on in the waiting area I check the timetable and await the arrival of the Chief. It's too early for *Wheel of Fortune* today, so I read my historic Appleton's railway guide. I love the adverts for hotels and ships printed on its pages, but so far this trip it hasn't delivered much help or insight to most of the cities I have been staying in. However, its main purpose is more spiritual than educational. Whenever I hold it I immediately feel like I have just become Phileas Fogg. I fantasise about smoking a pipe, wearing tweed and carrying a leather bag. In times before the mobile phone and the internet, books like this were all that you had to guide you through unfamiliar territory. Along with my Ball watch and my sheriff's badge, this book is a talisman to safe travel and

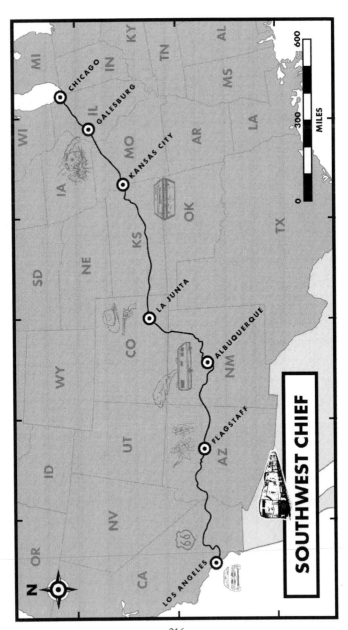

SOUTHWEST CHIEF

I treat it like a Bible. It takes up far too much room in my bag, but that's not the point.

The Chief is on time today, the sun is shining and by my calculation the good news is that I will be on board in time for lunch. In the distance, the 'ding ding' of the crossing signals that my Silver Streak is on the outskirts of town. Then the rumble of the diesel locos, and the engineer giving a toot on the horn on final approach. The lady who checked me in organises the sleeper passengers into a separate group and opens a door for us to go out of the waiting room onto the platform. Reaching the train means crossing the tracks of the Rail Runner line to Santa Fe, as here, like many smaller stations, there are no footbridges. I make a point of stopping and looking both ways before crossing. On average more than 500 people die each year on the tracks in the United States. People don't seem to like having to climb bridges.

For me it's lucky carriage 430 again, this time in roomette number 6. This is a good room assignment, as number 6 is away from the doors at the far end of the carriage and also away from the single top-deck toilet. Frankly I have yet to be in a roomette on a Superliner that I haven't liked, but if you're going to be a perfectionist, number 6 is a good one. I like number 2 as well, but for different reasons. It's located in the middle of the carriage, so feels smoother, is next to the coffee station and is just the right distance from the toilet. You also have the attendant opposite, so it's easy to get help or just have a quick chat. Viewliners are a different matter, though. Whilst the layout is quite similar, the whole commode-by-your-pillow thing is hideous.

The attendant is called Stephen, and as I'm one of the few people getting on the train here, he sorts me out a lunch reservation straight away. I'm already in a good mood today, but his spirits lift me even further. Nothing's just 'good' in his vocabulary; it's usually at least 'excellent'. If things are just okay, they're 'Allllllllright!' The only bad news he gives me is that the upstairs toilet is out of order, and we wait for a suitably qualified plumber to check it out. But time is running out and the Chief can't wait for something this trivial, so we pull out of Albuquerque without a fix. I wonder if that will be the only glitch for this journey.

The manager in the dining car recognises me and points out a table for me to sit at. The passengers in the dining car today look like a more mixed bunch than I'm used to seeing on the rails. Amongst the usual crowd of students, retirees and Mexican families on the move are a lot of Amish people. They stand out here by their distinctive and formal dress, almost a uniform to their way of life. Sitting opposite me are Elisa and Kemp, who are returning from Tijuana, where she goes once a year to visit a doctor. Amish people don't take planes as it's considered too modern, so the Chief is the best way for them to travel from Mexico back to their farmstead in Pennsylvania. The conversation is at first strange, but totally absorbing. It's not every day you get to interact with Amish people, and my entire knowledge of their way of life has been delivered through seeing the 1985 film *Witness*. It's the one where Harrison Ford plays the role of a policeman looking for a little Amish boy who has seen a murder in the bathroom of Philadelphia's railroad station. The Amish community didn't like the way that they were portrayed in the movie, and also complained that they were overrun with tourists in the locations where it was filmed. Despite the threat of a boycott, the film was a commercial success, and had it not been for *Beverly Hills Cop*, it would have been number one at the box office that year.

Elisa doesn't answer any of my questions herself. Kemp is the official spokesman for them as a couple. Instead she speaks to him in a form of German and he decides what to pass on to me in English. She sneaks a glance at me occasionally, but looks mostly at Kemp. It's very much a two-way exchange of information, though, as they are keen to find out from me what's going on in the world. They don't own a television, or even a mobile phone. Kemp asks me about American politics and their current president, explaining that they choose not to vote as that is outside their spiritual kingdom. They seem rather approving of my journey and ask me what I have learned so far, and what I hope to get out of the experience. These are deeper questions than I'm used to answering at lunchtime, and I do my best to answer them. What I can tell them is that the United States has become so misreported in the world's media, and that I've met many amazing people sitting in dining cars like this one. As for what I hope to get out of the experience, I hesitate to tell them that I hope to write a book about it, but I do say I'll be telling others about my journey.

It's always quiet after lunch on a long-distance train sleeper carriage. Passengers retreat into their own little worlds, some reading, some sleeping. I really enjoy this time of the day, as with no pressing engagements the time is yours to do as you want without being judged by anyone else. I recline the chair in my roomette and gaze out of the window at the landscape. I'm just about to doze off when Stephen pops by to book me in for dinner, handing me my little reservation ticket. No one has ever asked to see my reservation ticket, but it's nice to feel you have one. Amtrak doesn't seem to have any system for 'do not disturb'. Even on an aircraft you often get given a little sticker to wear in the hope that the crew will leave you alone. Here on board the sleeper, a closed door isn't left alone. But that said, at night-time there are few announcements and no one is going to bother you.

From time to time we come to a halt as another train passes, but other than that it's just a desert out there. The trains are mostly carrying freight, with different-looking, more industrial, locomotives hauling miles of mixed carriages. I have never been comfortable with being called a train spotter. I love the history of trains with names, but have no interest in their numbers. I remember briefly noting a few down in a little book in the 1970s but that was more about the class (type) of locomotive, rather than its individual number. Before the Second World War there were over 19,000 locomotives in the UK. By the 1950s, as post-war modernisation took place there was a frenzy to travel on steam trains and to explore many of their routes before they were finally consigned to history. Throughout the 1960s and 1970s although the steam trains might be gone, it was still a well-accepted hobby to hang out on the platform of your local railway station. They even sold speacial tickets to allow you to just be on the platform. For me, though, it was always about travelling on trains and, even better, a trip on a real train to the model shop to buy a model train.

In the United States they don't use the 'trainspotter' label. If you are really into trains then you are a 'railfan'. I quite like that. It sounds slightly more complimentary and less geeky. But an overly enthusiastic railfan is called a 'foamer' – literally foaming at the mouth – and if they have a camera, they become a 'rooster shooter'. If I'm going to be considered a true railfan I need to learn to recognise some of the trains. An afternoon game of I-Spy. The great thing about this is that it's much more fun to play here than back at home. Here, all the trains have nicknames, providing a vocabulary of rather amusing terms. If I could then learn to blend this in with a rudimentary knowledge of Amtrak speak, I might pass for a real railfan.

To give you an example of this rich dialect, if you see a refrigerated container train, it's called a juice train, or possibly a Trop if it's carrying that well-known brand of orange juice. A container train is a Pig Train, and a train carrying oil or flammable liquids is a Rolling Bomb. The locomotives have names often based on their shape or colour scheme. A Toaster is based on the look of an old Amtrak engine before the Mud Missile, and the orange-painted BNSF locomotive is called a Thunder Pumpkin. Before too long on the rails you might be able to spot the difference between a Big Mac and a Thunder Cow, or tell a Spongebob Squarecab from a Green Goat. Then you just need the confidence to drop these terms into casual railfan conversation.

When the next train approaches I note that it's a Pig Train being hauled by a Thunder Pumpkin. I have to go for it, despite having the apprehension of a schoolchild about to take a French language oral exam. Stephen's at the end of the corridor, so I wander down to the coffee station and look around the corner to the window, saying, 'Lots of Thunder Pumpkins coming the other way today.' I don't want to look too interested in his response, so I concentrate on making a cup of reasonable coffee. But I need not have worried. 'You bet, Matthew, enough pumpkins to make a pie, and then some.' I smile and nod. I've just passed my American railfan viva!

At just after 3pm we stop briefly at Las Vegas. Not the glitzy party capital in Nevada, but the small cowboy town in New Mexico, once home to characters like Jesse James, Billy the Kid and Wyatt Earp. Not only a lot of western films, but also parts of *No Country for Old Men* (2007), *Easy Rider* (1969), and *Convoy* (1978) were filmed here.

The quality of light is amazing in the observation lounge in the late afternoon. Indian reservations gradually give way to empty plains, some flooded, and in the distance the snow-covered mountains of Colorado. The tracks follow the river valleys as we begin to climb out of New Mexico. The train stops in Raton, the last station in New Mexico, just before 5pm, and we are invited by the conductor to stretch our legs. It's only down on this isolated platform that I can see how Amish the train has become. The Amish people don't waste a stop like the smokers or even the railfans like me. Instead they use it to take in fresh air and exercise. The women group in pairs at one end of the train whilst the men, now mostly dressed in black capes and straw hats, march up and down the whole length of the carriages with a measured pace. I leave them some extra space on the platform to march past. Stephen joins me to observe the prison yard-style exercise. He tells me this is quite normal on the Chief; it's the train he works on most weeks. Living in LA, he likes this run as he gets an 18-hour layover in Chicago before returning on the westbound service.

One long blast of the horn and the exercise period is

over. Passengers quickly return to their carriages like little fish retreating into a coral reef. A jolt, a slightly strained noise from the front of the train, and we are moving again. Farewell New Mexico, it's been a pleasure.

The locomotives are working hard now, pulling the train up the incline to the state line. The boundary is historic; it's the Raton Pass. The line is too steep for a lot of the freight trains, and as mentioned earlier this presents a significant issue in the funding and operation of a passenger service, as it has to be maintained solely by Amtrak. If it was able to pick and choose which services to run, it would probably abandon tracks like this and as a result cease to be a national rail operator. The top of the pass is at 7834 feet, and at this point the tracks pass through a tunnel into Colorado. The pass is also a major part of the story of settlement route between Kansas City and Santa Fe, originally laid by Captain William Becknell in 1821. In the 1870s this became part of the Colorado Railroad War. I don't think that I have ever heard of a railway war before, but one took place here between two rival railroad companies competing to build a route using the pass. Both the Atchison, Topeka and Santa Fe railway and the Denver & Rio Grande company wanted the prize of the only route into New Mexico. Due legal process failed, and railroad workers had to physically fight for the line. In the end the Atchison, Topeka and Santa Fe railway won the skirmish by hiring local gunfighters.

Colorado looks very different from New Mexico. Other than the trees and snow-capped mountains, the Chief passes through deserted mining towns that were once part of the Gold Rush and the Silver Boom, something that caused even more conflict between the railroad companies. But once silver became devalued the mines began to close, and the mill towns and coal towns that depended on them also had to shut down. All that was left were railway halts, which today look like archaeological projects rather than the thriving communities that were here 150 years ago. Stone foundations, dishevelled wooden cabins and rusted industrial machinery are all that remain.

If you spend a long time on a train you get used to what's normal and what might not be. The sounds, the rattles, the chatter over the PA. Like being in a ship at sea, or a plane in the air, your brain also normalises the swell or the turbulence and just notices any unusual events. You also sense normality in the behaviour of others. Judging by what I've just seen in the corridor there is definitely something unusual going on. At first the conductor passes through and has a quiet word with Stephen, and then I start to hear a few coded messages on the crew's intercom system. Given how the banter on the intercom is normally so open and fun, the use of code must signify something, but I just don't know what, as I have yet to crack this dialect of Amtrak speak.

The next scheduled stop is at Trinidad, Colorado,

towards 6pm, and as we approach the chatter over the intercom increases. This is a quick stop, so I'm not going to have time to stretch my legs, but little did I know getting out probably isn't going to be a good idea anyway. Trinidad looks like quite a big place, and after the ghost towns in the hills, it's my first glimpse of the American suburban way of life in a while. Once again, houses with pick-up trucks, inflatable swimming pools and big barbecues are set alongside the tracks. Stars and stripes fluttering outside well-tended front lawns with high wire fences. But as we reach the station the main activity is not cooking or for that matter any other leisure pursuits – it's law enforcement. As we slow down I can see the flashing blue lights of several police cars and vans waiting for us. The state police and cinder dicks on the platform are dressed in blue shirts and Mountie-style hats. Carriage 430 is towards the front of the train, so once I have passed the entourage there is no easy way for me to look back without getting off the train.

I have watched so many train films that this scene is not that unusual to me, but I have only encountered it once before in real life. It's how Inspector Mosely of the FBI hopes to catch Jack Walsh and Jonathan Mardukas in *Midnight Run*, and also the way the police plan to catch Roger Devereau in *Silver Streak*. The police have the element of surprise over their suspect, who can't see them ahead like a roadblock in the distance, so once at the station it's too late to escape.

There is silence over the intercom and no discernible noise inside the carriage. That might be a good thing; this isn't a shootout at least. We wait for a lot longer than the planned stop of a couple of minutes. Then finally a blast of the horn, the sound of slamming of doors further down the train, and we're rolling again. When I ask Stephen what's going on, I sense he is being economical with the truth: 'Everything's going to be alll-rrright, Matthew!' he tells me, and changing the subject, asks what time I would like to book dinner for.

When travelling on an aircraft, passengers expect to be told by the pilot what's going on, and thus the pilot usually feels an obligation to explain the reason for any delay or emergency, albeit in a professional and calming way. They can sometimes make even bad news sound okay. 'Ladies and gentlemen, boys and girls, the number three engine has fallen off and the co-pilot has food poisoning from the fish, but we hope to attempt an on-time landing at Chicago once we have passed through the thunderstorm.' There is a whole genre of comedy around this pilot–passenger relationship, too, perhaps best enshrined in the 1980 film *Airplane*. Who will ever forget Otto the inflatable autopilot?

On a train there seems to be less expectation of news or feedback from up front about events along the way. In the absence of this, my standard operating procedure is to go and ask what's going on in the dining car, where there are usually a couple of outlawed (off duty) staff. If they don't know, then it's a visit to the sightseeing lounge, the home to all gossip and rumour control aboard the train. That's how you find things out. In the dining car I find Tammy, one of the attendants. Looking a bit sheepish to be sharing the news with a passenger, she explains that they have had to de-board a coach passenger who refused to stop smoking. I reflect that they put on quite a reception for such a minor offence. Just imagine what the welcome party might look like for a proper criminal. I try to look shocked, but inwardly I'm thinking: Bravo! Smokers have been a constant annoyance in my rail travels in many other parts of the world. I'm all for stops to smoke on the platform, but to me smoking in the carriage is a wickedly selfish habit.

I like to eat a bit later than the average American does, so I try to opt for the last sitting of the service in the dining car. Tonight, it's early, at 7.30pm. With the make-up of passengers on this service, the dining car is almost empty by this time, just a few people finishing off their meals, so I find myself seated by myself. I choose the end table as I have discovered it is roomier than the rest for some reason. Tammy is still on shift and she finds me a little bottle of wine whilst I write up some notes at the table. As we pull into La Junta, Colorado, I order the signature steak, cooked medium and served with a baked potato, sour cream and green beans. You can't go wrong with a cooked-to-order steak in an Amtrak dining car. Some of the menu descriptions do puzzle me, though. The Angus burger I had at lunch was described as 'natural' and 'antibiotic and hormone free', like one on the menu back in Louisiana. It's a worrying thought that most burgers might be *un*natural, reminding me of that dystopian film *Soylent Green*, starring Charlton Heston and set in New York City in 2022, where food processors turn human corpses into nutritious processed food in the form of pills. Harry Harrison's book on which the film was based refers to them as Soylent Steaks. Another dish on the menu that catches my eye are the scrambled eggs at breakfast. They are advertised as being 'cage free'. I asked what that means here, and have a long lesson in the difference between a cage free, free range, and pasture-raised chickens.

La Junta is a small town on the high plain of south-eastern Colorado, and is the beginning of the stretch of line towards Kansas which is slower than other sections. It's commonplace to swap locomotives around here. The rail yard dates back to when the freight trains coming over the Raton Pass needed extra locomotives to help them climb the 3.5 per cent incline. But there isn't much else to see here any more. The original railway hotel has been replaced by an Amshack – a small brick building containing a waiting room and not much else – so I'm staying put in the dining car. The engineer announces that we're going to change some equipment here. The word 'equipment' suggests he might be going to swap fire axes, or get a new sandwich box, but what he actually means is big stuff, like carriages and locomotives. I hadn't factored this into my choice of mealtime, and all of a sudden we lose 'hotel power', leaving us in darkness with just the glow of the emergency backup lights. It's a shame we don't have candles on the tables in the dining car.

After half an hour, I order another little bottle of wine and hope Tammy won't judge me too harshly. She's not sure what's going on, and this doesn't seem to be at all normal. The kitchen can't cook without power, and after a while they send up a baked potato for me, but I tell chef that I'm happy to wait until they can cook my steak. The engineer decides to share some news, but it's in that impenetrable Amtrak language. What does 'we are waiting to resume functionality of the train' actually mean?

Before long it's just Tammy and myself left up top in the dining car. All the other passengers have retired to their rooms, so I invite her to join me for dinner – an unexpected bonus of our lack of power. We chat about all sorts of things. She has worked on the Chief for a long time, and it turns out that she has looked after some interesting characters in the dining car. What surprises me are some of the famous people who she has served dinner to. These include John Travolta, Ted Danson and Richard Dreyfus, but fortunately not at the same time. Can you imagine them having dinner together in the dining car? She's too discreet to reveal much about them, but I think she liked Ted Danson the most. I've never understood John Travolta. I suspect that dinner might have been a bit creepy. When the power eventually comes back on we're four hours behind schedule. My steak is a midnight feast, and I'm really grateful to the crew for cooking it, as they need to be up for breakfast in five or six hours. Wishing them well, I head back to my home in carriage 430.

I've got quite used to the small but comfortable space of the roomette. This might not be the Orient Express, but for one person it is both comfortable and practical. Once the bed is made you can't really do anything other than lie down. It is possible to stand up next to the door, but attempting to dress standing up requires manual dexterity and rhythm. I just about manage this tonight and lie back in my berth. I can't imagine sharing a compartment of this size, though. The upper berth is hard to get into, slightly narrower and makes the berth underneath more claustrophobic. From what I've seen of fellow passengers using it as double occupancy there is normally a long series of bribes to make someone opt for the upper berth, and once installed that person has to be waited upon by the person underneath. But in the sleeper carriage there are bigger rooms than the one I have. Amtrak bedrooms take up half the space on the upper deck and have a tiny bathroom and a permanent chair next to two berths, one above the other, the lower berth acting as a bench seat during the daytime. On the bottom deck of the carriage there is also a family room which is the complete width of the carriage. It has four beds but no ensuite. This is possible as there is no through corridor below.

Hollywood has at times taken some liberties with train interiors, but they can be hard to spot. In *Silver Streak*, George Caldwell has a room wide enough to have a bed across it, with a connecting door to Hilly Burns' room next door. James Bond has a similar room in *Live and Let Die*; it's even ensuite, as was the room of Jack Walsh in *Midnight Run*. That was where he handcuffed Jonathan 'The Duke' Mardukas. I suspect that these were all filmed inside real sleeper cars.

On the other hand, some directors choose to use a specially made carriage, often far wider than would be enable the train to pass other trains on the tracks. The 2017 remake of *Murder on the Orient Express* was shot in the UK with specially built carriages supposedly based on Pullman designs. They look lovely but I'm not convinced about the art deco interiors. Brad Anderson's 2008 film *Transsiberian* was also filmed on a specially constructed carriage that ran on tracks in Lithuania, and it looks incredibly real.

Sometimes the train can be authentic but the detail false. My favourite example of this was Daniel Craig and Eva Green on the fictitious train to Montenegro in the 2006 version of *Casino Royale*. Bond and Vesper sit in the dining car drinking a bottle of Chateau Angelus 1981 and enjoying some skewered lamb. But in the real world they were on a Czech Pendolino train that at the time of filming ran from Prague through Slovakia to Austria. I've had some interesting wines on trains, but at over €150 a bottle a Saint Emilion Grand Cru seems unlikely, especially served in the glasses used in the film. The observant will notice outside the train a station called Chur Ost, which does not exist in the real world: the Czech Republic was repurposed as Switzerland.

I close my eyes and fall asleep thinking about that sequence. The ultimate train fantasy of enjoying fine wine, silver service and good company in the dining car.

Silver Streak

Chapter Fourteen
Dead Man's Switch

When I emerge early for breakfast the following morning the dining car is nearly full. Amtrak don't run reservations at breakfast, but it normally sorts itself out over a three-hour window. Tammy is there to greet me and she seats me with a couple of elderly ladies who regard me with some suspicion and are keen to know what I'm up to. When she serves us coffee she points out a new and mysterious man who is now seated at the other end of the carriage. He joined the train in La Junta, apparently sent in by Amtrak to fix the problem last night. He must be the Amtrak equivalent of special forces, parachuted in to solve big problems with broken trains.

I enjoy my omelette whilst listening to the old girls discuss what they're going to do for the day. This revolves around extended sessions of gossip, knitting and a variety of word puzzles to keep their minds in peak shape between meals. I ask them what they know about our next stop, Kansas City. They tell me that it's famous for its fountains, its barbecue dry ribs, its jazz music, and being in Tornado Alley. I had forgotten about the tornados in these parts and immediately think of *The Wizard of Oz*, possibly the greatest film of all time. Thanking them as we pull into the station, I make my excuses and leave them to their knitting. Kansas City is a big station, and is the last big stop for the Chief on its run to Chicago. It's also a key location in the plot of *Silver Streak*. This is where George and Grover get on the train for the final time, having escaped custody in a stolen police car. Things start to get quite violent and far-fetched at this point in the film, but more of that later.

In carriage 430 Stephen has put my bed away, made some coffee, and has put his jacket on so he's ready for the stop. 'Here's the man!' he greets me with his characteristic smile. I wish I'd put my coat on too, as once he has the door open and the stepping stool placed down on the platform, I discover that it's quite fresh out there. At first it's hard to see much of the Chief, as the platform is obscured by huge concrete passenger staircases. Walking forwards along the train, I meet Kemp, who is now dressed in a black suit with matching cap. He's taking his obligatory march up and down the platform. I walk with him, struggling to get into the rhythm of his lengthy pace. Always polite, but not wanting to get too close to someone from the strange and corrupt modern world, he says 'Hello' and points to where the locomotives now stand. 'We have four today, two new ones in the night, and some more carriages also.' I can't see them all at first. The train is definitely longer, but silver blends into to silver, and they all look like one long silver streak of train from a distance. See what I did there? The only way to work it out is to walk up to the far end of the platform. Usually the baggage car is the final carriage before the locomotives, but when we reach it the train just keeps on going. There is a new cut of several unusual carriages next, and then no less than four Genesis locomotives. I've never seen carriages like these before. They are single-deck, like on a Viewliner – the same signature shape and design, yet somehow different. When the engineer said he was taking on some equipment at La Junta, I hadn't realised how much equipment he had in mind. It seems that we have become a hospital train, carrying equipment going in for repair or refurbishment. Kemp calls the moment for us to turn around and start the march back down the platform. Lingering and staring at the trains probably isn't allowed. When we get back to carriage 430 I part company with him and hang around by myself.

This city isn't as famous for its film locations as some of the other places I've visited, but staring at the concrete jungle behind the station it's hard for me to imagine that one of my favourite films was actually shot here. In 1973 Paramount Pictures released a film in black & white that was set in Kansas during the Great Depression. Starring Ryan O'Neal and his daughter Tatum O'Neil, it was titled *Paper Moon*. Orson Wells told Peter Bogdanovich, the director, that it was such a good name he could release just the title. Other than being filmed in black and white, it is perhaps best known for actress Tatum O'Neal, who at the time, aged just 10, became the youngest ever winner of an Academy Award, for her role as Addie Loggins. The Kansas City I see here at the station today has little of the small-town dustbowl feel created by the cinematography of *Paper Moon*.

I've got the Henri Mancini soundtrack to *Silver Streak* stuck in my mind. I think they call that an earworm. Most train films I can think of have soundtracks with set pieces for different moments of the film, and always one for when the train gets going again. It's not just *Silver Streak*, but *Midnight Run* and *Planes, Trains and Automobiles* too. As Stephen gets passengers back on board the engineer blasts the horn a couple of times. As it's a longer train, he must think it needs to be louder to reach people on the platform at the other end of the train. With the earworm playing in my head, we slowly gather momentum and pull out of Kansas City. I have the feeling that I should have stopped here for a couple days. The combination of jazz and barbecue sounds good, and maybe I might have persuaded the police to help me recreate the scene from *Silver Streak* where Grover busts through a road block. Looking at my watch and the timetable, I see we are about three hours behind schedule, but I have learned not to worry about things I can't be in control of, and unlike some of the other passengers I don't have a connection to make today.

Instead I relax and enjoy living in the moment. Time to sit back and watch the scenery.

I've circled a city on my map called Wichita. It's slightly south of where the tracks pass between Hutchinson, and Kansas City. You get a point if you remembered that this is the airport that Neal Page, played by Steve Martin, and John Candy as Del Griffith, get diverted to on their way to Chicago in *Planes, Trains and Automobiles*. After a night at a dodgy motel called the Braidwood Inn, they manage to get on a train to Chicago. But the train breaks down and they end up in Jefferson City before taking a bus on to St Louis. On the train, Neal and Del are seated in different coaches much to Neal's relief. The train has single-deck carriages with exterior paintwork that might pass for Amtrak in the 1980s. But in usual form, Amtrak did not want to be associated with one of its trains breaking down. Instead a 20-mile section of track had to be rented and carriages painted with fabricated logos. The locomotive in the film was branded Contrack. In the real world, then, they probably would have been getting on board the Southwest Chief.

Later in the morning we stop briefly at Fort Madison, Iowa, on the banks of the Mississippi. On the platform, talking to some people I haven't seen before, it seems we have picked up some vintage Amtrak carriages in La Junta that are going somewhere to be refurbished. You don't see them very often, and it makes the configuration of the Chief today very unusual. I have certainly never seen four locomotives hauling a train before.

The dining car has a bit of a country club feel about it at lunchtime. A lot of people now know each other and say hello to people they have met at past meals. Tammy points me to a table, and the community seating tradition of Amtrak once again rewards me with another chance to meet people from very different walks of life from my own. A bunch of high school kids have joined us at Kansas City and are travelling to Washington DC for a couple of days to see all the monuments and museums. The group are sat back in coach, keeping themselves to themselves, apart from a couple of girls who have decided to escape and try out the dining car. Tammy sits them with me rather than with the slightly creepy man wearing a bow tie sitting opposite. One of the girls is white American; the other, an exchange student, is Korean. I don't think they've been together long as some pretty basic questions are still being asked as they learn about each other's worlds. They order romaine salads – without dressing – whilst I tuck into another one of those antibiotic and hormone-free natural Angus burgers. They both eye up my phone and ask me what it is. I tell them I think it's an iPhone 4, which makes them smile and regard me with some pity. The American girl asks her Korean friend if she will move to America one day. She looks horrified at this possibility and says 'No!' with as much emotion as she probably feels she can express in a public place. I don't bother them with too many questions, choosing instead to enjoy the views of the river alongside the train as we cross over to the eastern side.

As a reminder that we have entered Illinois, we pass through Galesburg in the middle of the afternoon at about the time we were scheduled to arrive in Chicago. This is a railway town, and home to a big train depot (or 'dee-po' as someone in the carriage corrects me on my American). BNSF (Burlington North Santa Fe) is the largest employer in the city, and the line we are on also carries trains from other famous routes out of Chicago, like the California Zephyr. This is also where the original *Silver Streak* film was shot in just two days in September 1934. The only connection I know of to the film that remains today is the local football team – the Galesburg Silver Streaks.

Is it me, or are we speeding up? Illinois seems to be passing by my window much more quickly than the plains of Missouri. Perhaps the 'hogger' in the cab is trying to make up for lost time from last night. I only hope his watch is telling the right time. Eight and sand. Fortunately, since the 1970s, other than a few derailments, there have been few major incidents and no fatalities on the Chief.

Writers of train movie scripts don't have too many options for the narrative arc of their plots. Most of the time either the train arrives safely at its final destination and everyone's okay, or the train crashes in a spectacular fashion. But there is a hybrid version of this, where the train runs away and is about to crash but the protagonist manages to save the day. Sometimes there is also bomb on board, or a madman, sometimes both. In 2010 Tony Scott directed his final film, *Unstoppable*. It was his second train crash film, as he had directed the remake of *The Taking of Pelham 123* the year before. I think *Unstoppable* is a much better film than the credit it's been given by many of the critics. Interestingly the plot was written around a real runaway train and what is known as the CSX 8888 incident.

On 15th May 2001 an engineer was moving forty-seven cars of mixed freight, including some dangerous chemicals, in an Ohio rail yard. His CSX refurbished locomotive was number 8888, now notorious as the Crazy Eight. Noticing a misaligned switch on the rails ahead, he put on the airbrakes, set the throttle and hopped down to reset the switch before the train reached it. The first problem was that in the yard the air brakes were not connected and had no effect on the train. The second was that he had not actually set the throttle to dynamic braking, but to full power. Failing to get back on board, he could only watch helplessly as the now accelerating train, the Crazy Eight, together with all the cars it was pulling, headed up the line towards Toledo. It ran for 65 miles with no one at the controls. They tried to derail the train – the police even started shooting at it, trying to engage a fuel cut-off switch – but nothing worked. Eventually the crew of another train uncoupled their load, came out from a siding, caught up and recoupled with the back of the 8888 and slowed it enough for someone to climb aboard. An amazing real-life event that provided the perfect plot for a high-energy Tony Scott film.

Train warning systems, dynamic braking and throttle settings can be hard to absorb unless you are a qualified rail engineer. Not even a very extensive Hornby OO rail layout in your bedroom will prepare you for this. But the simplified concept of rail safety that we understand is the dead man's switch. The idea is that without someone with their foot on a pedal or hand on a lever, the train will stop. Modern trains still use this layer of safety, computers now asking the driver to confirm that they are at the controls, sometimes using pedals or buttons that need to be pressed every few seconds.

The Crazy Eight is still in service today but I'm fairly sure it won't be pulling the Southwest Chief across to Chicago any time soon. Instead, up front are two pairs of shiny General Electric P42DC Genesis locomotives. It's a double double head. A quadruple head? I ask the conductor about them. He's happy to explain that they are perfectly safe, and although they will shortly be replaced there is much life in them yet – and yes, they do have a working dead man's switch.

Silver Streak used this idea in the conclusion of its plot. Spoiler alert! After the big shoot out, baddy Richard

Devereau, played by Patrick McGoohan, gets into the locomotive where he kills the engineer and places a toolbox on the dead man's switch. George Caldwell and Chief Donaldson manage to injure Devereau, who ends up being decapitated by an oncoming train. With no one at the controls the train thunders through the outskirts of Chicago, where Caldwell and a steward manage to uncouple the passenger carriages in time to slow them safely. The locomotive speeds on ahead and ploughs right through Union Station, but everyone on board the train is saved. The film was mostly shot in Canada, as of course Amtrak didn't like the idea of a film about one of its trains taking out a couple of blocks of prime Chicago real estate.

I'm thinking about the practicality of uncoupling the carriages from a runaway Southwest Chief when Stephen walks past down the corridor. 'All-rrright Matthew?' he says looking in, in part-question, part-reassurance that I am all right. 'We'll be arriving in about an hour,' he says, which I can't understand as the timetable suggests we are two or even three hours behind. I ask him how that's possible, and he smiles and tells me the engineer has a special way of catching up. I'm not sure if this sounds like a good idea, but whether I like it or not, he's clearly not sparing the horses. He's set the four Genesis locomotives to the maximum line speed, and blasts the horn repeatedly as we speed through prairie towns.

Stephen fits right into my Silver Streak fantasies, and I

would like to think that were we involved in a shootout he would climb outside and uncouple our carriage from the bad guy in the engine with the toolbox on the dead man's switch. Whatever news he has he always shares with positive spin. If you told him the carriage was on fire the response would still be his signature 'All-rrright – no need to light the oven in the dining car tonight, then.' Or if you said that someone had been left behind, he might say 'All-rrright, more food for dinner.' Everyone needs a Stephen at times.

The Chief continues its sprint, and before long I think we might be in the outskirts of Chicago. I can't quite understand how we've managed to make up a couple of hours of time, but it seems we have. Water towers and old warehouses fill my window. Curving round the suburbs, the train begins to slow. Of course it's a good sign that the brakes are working, but at the same time a bad one as it means my adventure is drawing to an end. The buildings get taller and closer to the tracks, and then, saying goodbye to the daylight, the Chief dips underground into the bowels of Union Station. Gathering my belongings, I perform my usual double and triple checks that I have left nothing behind and head down the stairs one final time to the vestibule area on the lower deck.

Rather than smashing through the walls of the station, today the Silver Streak pulls up just short of the bumper, its four locos, elephant style, having pulled ten or more carriages. Walking towards the gate, I pause at the end of the platform and look back at the mighty Southwest Chief, now 2265 miles from where it had set out from LA two days earlier. The train looks magnificent under normal circumstances, but now with its quad head, it looks even mightier than usual.

A few of the crew that I know are waiting in a huddle to get their bags and finish work. I feel sad to have to say goodbye to them. Stephen grins at me and says he hopes to see me again soon, and Tammy tells me it's been great having me on the Chief.

Grover left Union Station driving a stolen mustard yellow Fiat X-19 that was on display in the concourse, dislodged from its stand by the train crash. The X-19 was quite a cool car back then, launched by Fiat in 1972, a convertible version available in America from early 1974. Styled by Bertone, its sharp angles, removable roof and retractable headlights were a bit space age for the time, especially in a car that cost less than $5000. It seems like an odd choice of car for Grover to drive, and must have been a valuable bit of product placement in 1976. In reality you couldn't just drive out the concourse at Chicago Union Station, but as the filming location was actually Toronto Union Station this wasn't a problem. What strikes me about the ending sequence of the film is how the passengers in the concourse walked right past CP4070, the wrecked locomotive. Can you imagine what the reaction would be in the event of such an accident today? The possibility of a fire or an explosion didn't seem to worry George and Hilly either, who embraced just in front of the loco as the closing credits began to roll.

Reunited with my bag and with no X-19 available to me, I take the escalator up to the Great Hall. In all its preserved glory, one thing that's notable by its absence is a departures board. If this were Europe or Asia, a whole wall would be devoted to a tennis court-sized display announcing arrivals and departures. But here today, beneath the original gold clock at the open plan information counter, is a modest display the size of a pool table. Its destinations remind me about the possibilities of future journeys by rail in the United States. Miami. Boston. Denver. Seattle. San Francisco. San Diego. Yes please! Just think of the film possibilities, too. Although it's time to go home, my American railroad adventures are far from over.

My American Airlines 787-9 Dreamliner takes off from O'Hare International Airport nearly two hours late, the sun setting behind the plane as it turns north-east to skirt over Quebec before reaching the North Atlantic.

Sipping on a glass of tepid white wine from a plastic cup that's smaller than I would have liked, I look through some of the photographs I have taken over the last few weeks on my phone. Pictures of some incredible places, and some amazing people smiling at me behind my viewfinder. I have a small lump in throat, remembering how warm and welcoming they have been to me. Some might argue that an adventure around America by train isn't as rugged or as exotic as crossing Siberia in the deep winter or even crossing the Indian subcontinent sleeping on a luggage rack, but that would be missing the point. The United States has allowed me to embrace its way of life in almost every way. Not much is hidden from the curious traveller, and with no real language barrier and many cultural similarities, it's possible to quickly embed oneself in the American dream. The United States has become misunderstood by much of the rest of world. Global news media is saturated with American politics, civil rights, violence and crime. But yet the vast majority of people I have shared my adventure with are intelligent, articulate and friendly. I met few of the stereotypes I had been used to seeing on my television.

All I can see out of the window from my seat is the wing, so instead I watch the path of the aircraft and the outside cameras from the little seat-back screen in front of me. I flick through the channels looking for something to watch. The problem I find these days is that there is so much content that you can spend more time trying to find something to watch than actually watching it. Amidst sitcom box sets, movies, cartoons, and earnest but misleading destination advice about visiting London, I find a news channel. The President of the United States is being interviewed about a new virus that he says comes from China. Apparently sixty people are now in hospital and it might be spreading in several states. 'It's going to be down close to zero,' he tells the reporter. 'That's a pretty good job we've done. It's going to disappear.' That's good news. I wouldn't like something like that to get in the way of my next adventure.

I hold the shiny Texas sheriff's badge from the hat shop in Houston in the palm of my hand and gently rub the lone star with my thumb. I promise myself I will return soon. I just don't know when 'soon' is going to be.

Learn to Speak Amtrack

All Aboard! - always shouted by the conductor before they signal for the doors to be closed by the car attendants. It's hard not to join in the fun and shout 'All aboard!' too … it can feel a bit like *Von Ryan's Express* at times with smoking stops on a long journey.

Amcan - a standard Amtrak passenger coach car, with rounded roof resembling a tin can.

Amfleet Coach Car - official name for standard single deck seated coach car. Comfy by European standards, with wide seats that compare with business class on an airline.

Amshack - small-town unmanned railway station.

Baggage - luggage. Occasionally weirdly used in the plural, as in 'your baggages must not be left in the corridor'. Travel with as little carry-on baggage as possible, as there might not be room for both you and your suitcase in a Roomette, but if it won't fit you can also store it on racks located on the lower level of a Superliner.

Baggage Car - a carriage just for storing bags, also sometimes called the Bag Dorm.

Baggage Master - the person responsible for getting the right bags on and off the baggage car at each major stop. Not all stops have a baggage service, so if yours is a small stop you might have to store your bags in your sleeper or coach car.

Bedroom - a room with two beds and an ensuite toilet. This as luxurious as it gets on an Amtrak train, and you can imagine being in a classic train film like *Silver Streak* whilst you dress for dinner. No one else will be dressing for dinner, though.

Bed - it's a bed, not a berth. In a Roomette, the lower bed is much better than the upper one. It's bigger and more padded. If you are sharing, negotiate well with your partner.

Bedroom Suite - Two twin Bedrooms with separate ensuite rooms joined by an interconnecting door. The sort of room James Bond would have if he were travelling on Amtrak.

Big Mac – nickname for the SD80MAC locomotive.

Brakeman - old-fashioned name for the Conductor, sometimes still used to describe the person responsible for the running of the train.

Buggy - if you book a Red Cap service you get a lift to the door of your carriage in an electric buggy similar to one used at an airport.

Bumper - the barrier at the end of the line. For example, Conductor: 'That's us up on the bumper at 12.36.'

Business Class - upgraded coach class car with inclusive benefits like food and wi-fi. Most business people in America travel by plane, so not in great demand.

Café Car - the lower deck of the Observation Car has a bar and snack shop with a few tables. Open longer hours than the restaurant and mainly serving passengers in coach class. Unlimited supply of ice and often run by staff member who has trained at the Amtrak equivalent of a holiday camp.

Car - a rail carriage, not a road-based car (that would be a 'vee-hicle').

Cinder Dick - railroad police, derived from walking on cinder ballast.

Coach Attendant - confusingly can also be called a Conductor. Responsible for rooms on sleeper cars and anything you might need during your time on the train.

Coach Class - regular daytime seated car that in Amtrak coach has comfortable seats. The Viewliner and Superliner versions feel like first class compared to many European trains, but have no inclusive benefits like food or drink.

Coffee Station - found in the middle of the top deck on a Superliner or at the end of the dining car in a Viewliner. Reasonable freshly brewed coffee is always available.

Community Seating - the dining car policy is to place diners together at a reserved dining time. There is no choice in this matter. By staggering arrivals into groups, the staff can seat people together in one half of the car and serve their meals at the same time. Meanwhile the other half can be cleared and readied for a second sitting. Most Americans eat early, so if you want more peace and personal space you will usually find that by 19.45, the last sitting, the dining car will be half-empty.

Conductor - crew member responsible for management and ticketing on a regular train.

Cut - a group of carriages coupled together.

Dead Man's Switch - pedal or device to prove that the locomotive has an Engineer, conscious and awake, in the cab.

De-board - to get off the train.

Depot ('Dee-po') - often a large junction that may well also be a station. May involve backing into the platform and lots of tooting of the horn.

De-train - same meaning as 'de-board'.

Dining Car - a carriage where meals are served at specific times for breakfast, lunch and dinner. Reservations are usually required.

Dining Car Reservation - alien to the European traveller, a system of seating people at set times for meals. Taken in advance by a service attendant in the sleeper coaches where meals are included.

Double Spot - Not a snooker or pool word. This is where the train is longer than the platform, and it will stop twice to let the passengers from every carriage De-board.

Dorm Car - Superliner car which is half used for staff accommodation (lower deck) and connects to baggage car. This isn't Hogwarts, though. See also Transition Car.

Dynamic Braking - using the motors to generate electrical power whilst slowing the momentum of the train.

Eight and Sand - a phrase to wish crews well, derived from the highest power setting on the throttle and sand to prevent wheel-slip.

Elephant Style - group of locomotives all facing in the same direction, as in a circus parade. Also known as N2A, or nose to ass.

Engineer - the train driver. It's part of the railroad history that the Engineer is responsible for all aspects of the train.

Equipment - term to describe the locomotive and or its carriages.

Family Room - four-bedded room suitable for two adults and two children on lower deck of sleeper car; lots of space, but no ensuite.

Fireman - the second Engineer, or driver. They work in 12-hour shifts.

Flexible Dining Menu - Microwave meals on trains east of the Mississippi. The worst thing to happen to Amtrak for a long time.

Foamer - an overly enthusiastic train spotter, who literally foams at the mouth.

Full Meal Service - Freshly cooked food from the original menu prepared in the kitchen of a Superliner dining car.

Gate - entry point to platform, sometimes where tickets are checked.

Going to Beans - taking a meal break.

Hogger - another word for the Engineer.

Hospital Train - a train carrying carriages and locomotives to a repair shop.

Hotel Power - electricity generated by the locomotive to power the carriages.

IC - the intercom, not the PA. The private communication system between carriage attendants for the resolving problems and telling jokes.

Lead Service Attendant - the person who supervises service in the dining car. Often heard on the PA announcing dining times and moving people on and off the wait list, depending on his or her mood. Sometimes called the Steward.

Menu Specials - Amtrak Culinary Advisory Team dishes are interesting-looking dinner choices on the restaurant menu. I have never found them actually available to order, though, so don't get too excited by reading about them.

Mud Missile - unfortunate nickname for the common Amtrak GE Genesis locomotive as a result of a 1990s disaster.

Observation Car - a two-level car with a mix of seating and panoramic windows on the upper deck, and a bar and café below. Usually the social centre of the train and a good place to chat with fellow passengers.

Outlawed - Crew members who have reached the maximum number of permitted hours on their shift.

PA - Public address system. Used for all sorts of passenger communication, including dinner reservations and occasional banter.

Parlour Car - see Dining Car. More specifically the part of the dining car where the on-duty service attendant sits and puts together the community seating plan.

Pig Train - train carrying containers on flatcar trailers.

Quiet Car - unreserved coach car with a no-noise, no-phone policy. Mainly seen on single-deck trains on more business-orientated routes.

Railfan - train spotter.

Redcap - porter who deals with checked luggage. All big bags are checked in as at an airport. The redcaps then transfer them to the baggage car.

Restroom - the toilet. On Superliners there is one upstairs and three downstairs per sleeper car. On a Viewliner only in the sleeper rooms and coach cars.

Rolling Bomb - a train carrying cars with flammable liquids.

Roomette - small compartment with two chairs that converts into an upper and lower berth at night. Cosy for one, a bit tight for two. It's not a cabin or a compartment.

Rooster Shooter - railfan or train spotting photographer.

Runaround - detaching the locomotive from one end of the train and moving it to the other for the return journey.

Service Attendant - person who serves meals and drinks in the dining car, also called a Steward.

Shower Room - one per sleeper car, located on its lower deck.

Sightseeing Lounge - see Observation Car.

Sleeper Car - car made up of overnight accommodations - roomettes, family rooms and bedrooms. Sometimes also called a Sleeperette.

Sleeping Car Lounge - if you are travelling on a route using the Flexible Dining Menu then the Dining Car seating area is repurposed into a simple lounge where you can eat the food you've chosen.

Smoke Stop - longer stops where baggage is being handled and the conductor invites passengers to stretch their legs on the platform. Also called 'comfort stops'.

Superliner - a two-level long-distance Amtrak car used on some routes. Deeply impressive.

Surfliner - same as a Superliner but a sign that you are in California. Small surfboards and saxophones are also allowed in the coach cars.

Switch - points.

Thunder Pumpkin - nickname for orange BNSF locomotive. BNSF is the largest freight network in North America.

Toaster - old-fashioned square-looking Amtrak locomotives that spark a lot. General Electric made these as well as various household appliances.

Transition Car - car set aside for use by crew, usually a Sleeperette. It has twin decks at the Superliner end, and at the other it's single height to connect to the baggage car.

Truck - the unit of wheels, suspension and brakes, also known as a bogie.

Viewliner - single level/deck version of Superliner used on some Amtrak routes

Filmography

Film locations are included where relevant to places visited on the journey, together with a few thoughts.

1941. 1979. [Film]. Steven Spielberg. Dir. USA: Universal Pictures. Filmed in Los Angeles, California. Santa Monica Pier appears throughout the movie.

3.10 to Yuma. 2007. [Film]. James Mangold. Dir. USA: Lionsgate. Filmed in and around Santa Fe, New Mexico. Bonanza Creek Ranch and Ghost Ranch feature extensively and Russell Crowe gets by far the best hat.

633 Squadron. 1964. [Film]. Walter Grauman. Dir. UK: United Artists. The aerial scenes were shot mainly in Scotland, and the base scenes were filmed at RAF Bovingdon. The pub is The Three Compasses in Aldenham, England.

Airplane. 1980. [Film]. Jim Abrahams, David Zucker &

Jerry Zucker. Dir. USA: Paramount Pictures. Surreal slapstick comedy and, unofficially, one of the funniest films of all time.

Apocalypse Now. 1979. [Film]. Francis Coppola. Dir. USA: United Artists. Simply one of the best movies ever made. The making of the film is almost as interesting as the film itself.

Apollo 13. 1995. [Film]. Ron Howard. Dir. USA: Universal Pictures. Partly set in Houston, Texas, but actually filmed mainly in the studio in Los Angeles, California. Howard was offered Building 30 at the Johnston Space Center, but instead chose to reconstruct this in the studio. The Florida motel is the Safari Inn, 1911 Olive Boulevard, Burbank, and the astronaut apartments were in the Ambassador Hotel, 3400 Wiltshire Boulevard, Los Angeles.

A-Team, The. 1982–85. [TV]. Frank Lupo/Stephen Cannell. Creators. USA: MCA TV. Filmed at Universal Studios, Universal City, California. An implausible amount of shooting firearms for no one to be seen actually getting shot.

Better Call Saul. 2015–20. [TV]. Vince Gilligan/Peter Gould. Creators. USA: AMC. Filmed on location in Albuquerque, New Mexico. Several locations are shared with *Breaking Bad*.

Beverley Hills Cop. 1984. [Film]. Martin Brest. Dir.

USA: Paramount Pictures. Filmed in Detroit, Los Angeles and Pasadena. Santa Monica Boulevard appears in the sequel, Beverly Hills Cop II (1987).

Big. 1988. [Film]. Penny Marshall. Dir. USA: 20th Century Fox. Filmed in New York City, New York. The Zoltar scene was filmed at the Ross Dock Picnic Area on the Palisades Interstate Park, NY.

Blues Brothers, The. 1980. [Film] John Landis. Dir. USA: Universal Pictures. Filmed in and around Chicago, Illinois. The prison scene was shot at the Joilet Correctional Center, south of the city.

Blue Peter. 1958–Present. [TV]. John Hunter Blair. Creator. UK: BBC Television. Ground-breaking, and also the longest-running children's television show in the world.

Bonanza. 1960–73. [TV]. David Dotort. Creator. USA: NBC Films. Filmed in Warner Studios, but also on location in the San Jacinto Mountains, California, and Lake Tahoe, Nevada, the setting for the Ponderosa Ranch.

Boyz n the Hood. 1991. [Film]. John Singleton. Dir. USA: Columbia Pictures. Set on Cimarron Street and surrounding locations in south central Los Angeles, California.

Breaking Bad. 2008–13. [TV]. Vince Gilligan. Creator.

USA: Sony Pictures Television. Filmed on location in Albuquerque, New Mexico. Iconic locations include Twisters at 4257 Isleta Boulevard, the Octopus carwash at 9516 Circle NE, and the Crossroads Motel at 1001 Central Avenue.

Butch Cassidy and the Sundance Kid. 1969. [Film]. George Roy Hill. Dir. USA: 20th Century Fox. The railway robberies were filmed on the Durango–Silverton railway, Colorado, and also Santa Fe, New Mexico. The river leap was set near Durango, but completed in Malibu, California.

Casino Royale. 2006. [Film]. Martin Campbell. Dir. UK: Sony Pictures. The Czech train operating between Prague, Slovakia and Austria is used on Bond's journey from Switzerland to Montenegro.

Charlie's Angels. 1976–81. [TV] Ivan Goff, Ben Roberts Creators. USA: ABC. Trashy 1970s series that looks quite inappropriate today. It only really just passed as family viewing.

Cheers. 1982–93. [TV]. Glen and Les Charles, James Burrows. Creators. USA: Paramount/CBS Television Distribution. The Boston bar where everybody knows your name.

Clockwise. 1986. [Film]. Christopher Morahan. Dir. UK: Universal Pictures. John Cleese misses his train to Norwich. A rail travel nightmare of mine to this day.

Convoy. 1978. [Film]. Sam Peckinpah. Dir. USA: United Artists. Part filmed in Las Vegas, New Mexico where the brass band plays in the town square and the Plaza Hotel.

Crimson Tide. 1995. [Film]. Tony Scott. Dir. USA: Buena Vista Pictures. The U.S. Navy refused to help with filming owing to the plot. The French Navy allowed filming instead.

Dallas. 1978–91. [TV]. David Jacobs. Creator. USA: Warner Brothers Television. 357 episodes made it the longest-running prime time drama in American television history.

Dam Busters, The. 1955 [Film]. Michael Anderson. Dir. UK: Pathe/Warner Brothers. Two versions of this film are now shown on television in different countries/channels, one of which is censored, mainly owing to the name of Guy Gibson's dog.

Das Boot. 1981. [TV film]. Wolfgang Petersen. Dir. Germany: Columbia Pictures. The most expensive German film ever made at the time of production. The outdoor model of the submarine was shared during filming with Steven Spielberg who was making *Raiders of the Lost Ark*.

Die Hard with a Vengeance. 1995. [Film]. John McTierman. USA: 20th Century Fox. Filmed in locations across Manhattan. The taxi scene sequence originates in Central Park.

Dirty Harry. 1971. [Film]. Don Siegel. Dir. USA: Warner Brothers. Filmed on location in San Francisco, California. Harry Callahan favoured the model 29 Smith & Wesson .44 magnum – he called it 'the most powerful handgun in the world', but of course that's no longer true.

Dogtown and Z-Boys. 2001. [Film]. Stacy Peralta. Dir. USA: Sony Pictures. Filmed on location in Venice Beach and Santa Monica, California.

Easy Rider. 1969. [Film]. Dennis Hopper. Dir. USA: Columbia Pictures. The parade sequence was filmed in Las Vegas, New Mexico.

Fawlty Towers: The Psychiatrist *and* Gourmet Night. 1979. [TV] John Cleese/Connie Booth. Creators. UK: BBC.

Ferris Bueller's Day Off. 1986. [Film]. John Hughes. Dir. USA: Paramount Pictures. Filmed on location in Chicago, Illinois. The Willis Tower (Sears Tower) and 333 Wacker Drive appear prominently.

Fletch. 1985. [Film]. Michael Ritchie. Dir. USA: Universal Pictures. Filmed in Beverly Hills and Santa Monica, Los Angeles, as well as in Utah. Central to the plot is drug dealing on the beach underneath Santa Monica Pier.

Fugitive, The. 1993. [Film]. Andrew Davis. Dir. USA:

Warner Brothers. Filmed on locations across Chicago. The train crash was filmed at Dillsboro, North Carolina.

Girl on the Train, The. 2016. [Film]. Tate Taylor. Dir. USA: Universal Pictures. Scenes set in Grand Central Station and the Oyster Bar. The shots out of the train took place in White Plains, Hastings-on-Hudson, and Irvington, New York State.

Godfather Part II, The. 1974. [Film] Francis Ford Coppola. Dir. USA: Paramount Pictures. The film won six Oscars and is arguably even better than the original movie in the trilogy.

Goliath. 2016. [TV]. David Kelley/Jonathan Shapiro. Creators. USA: Amazon Studios. Filmed at locations around Los Angeles, California. The Ocean Lodge Hotel and Chez Jay are on Ocean Avenue, Santa Monica. Union Station is also used as a location in Season 2.

Grange Hill. 1978–08. [TV]. Phil Redmond. Creator. UK: BBC Television. After school television in a new gritty style thanks to new kid on the block Phil Redmond.

Groundhog Day. 1993. [Film]. Harold Ramis. Dir. Columbia Pictures. Started a new genre of comedy fantasy film. Shot mainly in Woodstock, Illinois.

Happy Days. 1974–84. [TV]. Garry Marshall. Creator. USA: CBS. 255 episodes of a family sitcom about a cool biker who lives above the garage of the family home. A young Ron Howard co-stars, before making his name as a film director and producer.

Hawaii Five-O. 1968-80. [TV]. Leonard Freeman. Creator. USA: CBS. Just two episodes filmed in LA. Mostly shot on location in Hawaii. Jack Lord stars as Steve McGarrett, complete with cool hairstyle and a dark suit.

Heat. 1995. [Film]. Michael Mann. Dir. USA: Warner Brothers. Filmed around Los Angeles, California. The robbery is set on Venice Boulevard at Convention Center Drive beneath the Santa Monica Freeway.

High Chaparral, The. 1967–71. [TV]. David Dortort. Creator. USA: NBC Films. Mainly filmed around Tucson, Arizona.

Hunt for Red October, The. 1990. [Film]. John McTiernan. USA: Paramount Pictures. Not filmed anywhere near a real submarine, but instead on the Paramount backlot in L.A.

John Craven's Newsround. 1972–Present. [TV]. Edward Barnes & John Craven. Creators. UK: BBC Television. The latest news specially repackaged for kids.

K-19: The Widowmaker. 2002. [Film] Katheryn Bigelow. Dir. USA: Paramount Pictures. Filmed on real submarines in Canada.

Lethal Weapon. 1987. [Film]. Richard Donner. Dir. USA: Warner Brothers. Filmed at locations around Los Angeles, California, including the International Tower at Long Beach and Dockweiler state beach, Playa del Rey.

Little House on the Prairie. 1974–83. [TV]. Laura Inglis Wilder. Creator. USA: NBC. 204 episodes of Saturday afternoon family entertainment syndicated around the world.

Live and Let Die. 1973. [Film]. Guy Hamilton. Dir. USA: United Artists. Filmed in New York City, New Orleans, and also in Jamaica. The Fillet of Souls is at 834 Chartres Street, New Orleans, and in NYC is was set on 94th Street and 2nd Avenue. The riverboat chase was filmed in the Louisiana bayous.

Local Hero. 1983. [Film]. Bill Forsyth. Dir. UK: 20th Century Fox. Filmed on location in Scotland, mainly in Pennan on the Aberdeenshire coast. The Knox Oil and Gas headquarters is One Shell Plaza, 910 Louisiana Street, and JPMorgan Chase Tower, Houston, Texas. The testing lab was filmed at the Johnson Space Center, Houston, Texas.

Looney Tunes. 1949–2018. [TV]. Chuck Jones/ Michael Maltese. Creators. USA: Warner Brothers. The home of Wile E. Coyote and the Road Runner.

Magpie. 1968–80. [TV]. Lewis Rudd & Sue Turner.

Creators. UK: Freemantle. A version of *Blue Peter* on the other channel, for cooler kids.

Man on Fire. 2004. [Film]. Tony Scott. Dir. USA: 20th Century Fox. Mostly filmed in Mexico City, but scenes also filmed at the Juárez/El Paso border.

Maverick. 1957-62. [TV]. Roy Huggins. Creator. USA: Warner Brothers Television. The show that made James Garner, but in the third season he was replaced by Roger Moore.

Miami Vice. 1984-90. [TV]. Michael Mann. Creator. USA: NBC. Redefined the look and style of TV crime drama in the 1980's.

Midnight Run. 1988. [Film]. Martin Brest. Dir. USA: Universal Pictures. Filmed in Los Angeles, California, and New York City, New York. The train sequence is shot at Flagstaff train station, Arizona. The river sequence was actually shot in New Zealand.

Mr Benn. 1971–72. [TV]. David McKee. Creator. UK: BBC Television. One of the greatest ever kids' TV shows, and constant provider of travel inspiration to me.

Murder on the Orient Express. 2017. [Film]. Kenneth Branagh. Dir. USA: 20th Century Fox. Filmed at Longcross Studios in the United Kingdom with replica trains and lots of snow.

No Country for Old Men. 2007. [Film]. Joel and Ethan Coen. Dirs. USA: Miramax Films. Filmed in New Mexico and Mexico. The shoot-out motel is the Desert Sands, 5000 Central Avenue SE, in Albuquerque. The other motel is the Regal Hotel in Las Vegas, New Mexico.

North by Northwest. 1959. [Film]. Alfred Hitchcock. Dir. USA: Metro-Goldwyn-Mayer. Like *Silver Streak*, another film with a biplane, that some say inspired the helicopter chase in *From Russia with Love*. Several scenes were filmed in NYC, including Grand Central Station.

Octopussy. 1983. [Film]. John Glen. Dir. UK: MGM/UA Entertainment. The railway scenes were shot at the Nene Valley Railway in Peterborough, England.

Paper Moon. 1973. [Film]. Peter Bogdanovich. Dir. USA: Paramount Pictures. Set in several Kansas towns including the rail depot at Gorham.

Planes, Trains and Automobiles. 1987. [Film]. John Hughes. Dir. USA: Paramount Pictures. Filmed in NYC, New York, Chicago and around Illinois. The Chicago L scene is La Salle–Van Buren Station. The railroad station is South Drayton, Buffalo, NY. Wichita, Kansas, is actually Braidwood, Illinois. The Braidwood Inn is actually the Sun Motel.

Point Break. 1991. [Film]. Katheryn Bigelow. Dir. USA: 20th Century Fox. Johnny Utah meets Tyler Endicott at

Neptune's Net on the Pacific Coast Highway, west of Malibu. Some of the beach sequences were filmed at nearby Leo Carrillo State Beach.

Prisoner, The. 1967. [TV]. Patrick McGoohan and George Markstein. Creators. UK: MGM-British Studios.

Professionals, The. 1977–81. [TV]. Brian Clemens. Creator. UK: London Weekend Television. Famed for 70s men's fashion, cool cars and firing ludicrous firearms ineffectively at the bad guys.

Rockford Files, The. 1974–80. [TV]. Roy Huggins/ Stephen Cannell. Creators. USA: Universal Television. Filmed around Los Angeles, California. Jim Rockford's trailer was at 2354 Beach Boulevard and Paradise Cove, Malibu. Malibu Pier is used in the opening credits sequence.

Rocky III. 1982. [Film]. Sylvester Stallone. Dir. USA: United Artists. Filmed in Los Angeles, California. Rocky and Apollo run along the beach to the soundtrack of 'Eye of the Tiger' by Survivor at Santa Monica Pier.

Roobarb and Custard. 1974. [TV]. Grange Calveley. Creator. UK: BBC Television. Always the last programme before the evening news in the United Kingdom, voiceover by the late great Richard Briers.

Sicario. 2015. [Film]. Denis Villeneuve. Dir. USA: Lionsgate. Much of the filming was in Albuquerque,

New Mexico and the film was partly set in Juárez.

Silver Streak, The. 1934. [Film]. Tommy Atkins. Dir. USA. Filmed in Galesburg, Illinois. Union Pacific refused to supply their shiny new passenger train.

Silver Streak. 1976. [Film]. Arthur Hiller. Dir. USA: 20th Century Fox. Although set on a train between Los Angeles and Chicago, it was almost entirely filmed in Ontario, Canada.

Simpsons, The. 1989–Present. [TV]. Matt Groening. Dir. USA: Fox.

Six Million Dollar Man, The. 1973–78. [TV] Martin Caidin. Creator. USA: ABC. Essential viewing in the mid-1970s, and encouraged children everywhere to practise their slow-motion running skills.

Southern Comfort. 1981. [Film]. Walter Hill. Dir. USA: 20th Century Fox. Filmed on location in Louisiana, mainly in the Caddo Lake area.

Soylent Green. 1973. [Film]. Richard Fleischer. Dir. USA: Metro-Goldwyn-Mayer. The 'Soylent Steaks' from the book did not make it into the film.

Speed. 1994. [Film]. Jan de Bont. Dir. USA: 20th Century Fox. Shot on California's Interstate 105 and 110. The bus jump was of course, CGI.

Space 1999. 1975-77. [TV]. Gerry and Sylvia Anderson. Creators. UK: ITC Entertainment. Saturday morning television with American money from ITC that made *Doctor Who* look very much on a budget in comparison.

Spy Who Loved Me, The. 1977. [Film]. Lewis Gilbert. Dir. UK: United Artists. Pivotal James Bond film with Roger Moore at his best, although without help from any trains in this movie.

Star Wars: Episode IV – A New Hope. 1977. [Film]. George Lucas. USA: 20th Century Fox. Mainly shot at Elstree Studios in Borehamwood, England, only a couple of miles from where I grew up.

Straight Outta Compton. 2015. [Film]. F. Gary Gray. Dir. USA: Universal Pictures. Filmed in Compton, Los Angeles, California.

Taken 2. 2012. [Film]. Olivier Megaton. Dir. France: Europacorp. The end sequence is shot at the Malibu Farm Pier Café, Malibu Pier, California.

Taking of Pelham 123, The. 2009. [Film]. Tony Scott. Dir. USA: Sony Pictures. Filmed in New York City, New York. Locations include Grand Central Station, Manhattan Bridge, and various locations in Brooklyn, Queens and the Bronx.

Terminator, The. 1984 [Film]. James Cameron. Dir. USA: Orion Pictures. Filmed in Los Angeles, California.

The Alamo gun shop was filmed at 14329 Victory Boulevard at Tyrone Avenue, Van Nuys in the San Fernando Valley.

Terminator 2: Judgment Day. 1991. [Film]. James Cameron. Dir. USA: TriStar Pictures. Filmed in Los Angeles, California. The shopping mall scene is Santa Monica Place, Broadway and Third Street. The flood channel chase sequence was shot at Bull Creek, San Fernando Valley. Dyson's house is set on the Pacific Coast Highway, west of Malibu.

Them! 1954. [Film]. Gordon Douglas. Dir. USA: Warner Brothers Pictures. Filmed in Los Angeles, California, and the Mojave Desert, California. The ants' final nest is in a spillway of the Los Angeles river between the First and Seventh Street Bridges, east of L.A.

Tiswas. 1974–82. [TV]. Peter Tomlinson. Creator. UK: ITV Studios. Saturday morning children's television show that had no educational value whatsoever. Banned in my household.

Traffic. 2000. [Film]. Steven Soderbergh. Dir. USA: USA Films. Filmed in California, New Mexico, Ohio, Texas, Mexico and Washington DC. General Salazar's HQ is a farm near El Paso, Texas.

Transsiberian. 2008. [Film]. Brad Anderson. Dir. UK: Icon Film Distribution. Mainly filmed in Lithuania using a specially built carriage running on real tracks.

Triangle. 1981. [TV]. Bill Sellars. Creator. UK: BBC Television. To this day, some of the worst television ever produced.

Two and a Half Men. 2003–15. [TV]. Chuck Lorre & Lee Aronsohn. Creators. USA: Warner Brothers Television. Charlie Harper's house is supposedly on Colony Road, Malibu, California.

U-571. 2000. [Film]. Jonathan Mostow. Dir. USA: Universal Pictures. The real U-505 is now preserved in the Museum of Science and Technology, Chicago.

Unforgiven. 1992. [Film]. Clint Eastwood. Dir. USA: Warner Brothers. Filmed in Alberta, Canada, rather than Wyoming, where most of the story is set.

Unstoppable. 2010. [Film]. Tony Scott. Dir. USA: 20th Century Fox. Filming took place in various parts of Ohio and Pennsylvania. Ohio was home to the real-life CSX 8888 incident.

Untouchables, The. 1987. [Film]. Brian De Palma. Dir. USA: Paramount Pictures. Filmed in Chicago, Illinois. The set piece shootout is on the stairs of the Great Hall of Union Station on the Canal Street side, 210 South Canal Street.

Von Ryan's Express. 1965. [Film]. Mark Robson. Dir. USA: 20th Century Fox. Mainly filmed in northern Italy, but the closing sequence was shot in Andalucía, Spain.

The railway station is really Roma Ostiense, rather than Firenze Santa Maria Novella.

Wall Street. 1987. [Film]. Oliver Stone. Dir. USA: 20th Century Fox. Filmed on the streets of New York City where 'greed is good'.

Waltons, The. 1972–81. [TV]. Earl Hammer Jr. Creator. USA: Warner Brothers Television. 221 episodes of life in rural Virginia.

Wheel of Fortune. 1975–Present. [TV]. Merv Griffin. Creator. USA: CBS Media. One of the highest rated programmes on U.S. television. A hangman-meets-roulette-based game.

Wild Geese, The. 1978. [Film]. Andrew McLaglen. Dir. UK: Rank. Filmed in Twickenham, England and the Northern Transvaal. As close as McLaglen got to making his very own *Where Eagles Dare*.

Witness. 1985. [Film]. Peter Weir. Dir. USA: Paramount Pictures. Shot on location in Philadelphia and the towns of Lancaster, Strasburg and Parkesburg.

Wizard of Oz, The. 1939. [Film]. Richard Thorpe, Victor Fleming, King Vidor. Dirs. USA: Loew's Inc. Filmed on an MGM lot in Culver City, California. One of the most important films ever made.

Silver Streak

Acknowledgements

I would like to thank everyone who encouraged me to write this book. Many curries were consumed developing thoughts and getting ideas from inspirational people. Without the encouragement of Keith Parsons, I would not yet have written a single word, and without the gentle guidance of Mark Hudson, I probably would not have chosen America for the subject of this book – what a mistake that would have been. For the original film inspiration, I'm privileged to have been a pupil and small soldier serving under the late Lieutenant-Colonel Timothy Elford OBE.

I am indebted to my production team. My editor, Caroline Petherick, has once again kept me on the straight and narrow and helped me with the structure of this book. Olga Tyukova found the time to draw the lovely train illustrations, and Colin and Jake at NDC came up with a wonderful book design as well as a whole new atlas of rail maps. My thanks also to the early reader team – Rob Woodcock, Ruby Golding and Geoff Price.

John Blower helped me pull together the 'cunning plan' on the ground, saving me a vast amount of time, and Sheila Manzano worked tirelessly trying to get the attention and support of Amtrak, which I so wanted to put at the heart of this story. Ahead of the trip Nick Wiseman and Malika Brown at the Ball Watch Company joined my team of supporters. I'm very grateful to them for believing that interesting stories can come from the heritage of the American railroad.

Off the rails, it lifted my spirits to have people to help me find the stories I was looking for in the places that I visited. In Chicago, James Devlin was my special advisor on all matters beer and wings. He also taught me all I that know about the NFL. To the CTC Steppers in New Orleans for looking after me in their second line. Los Angeles would not have been nearly as interesting without the help of Josh Weinstein on the trail of Jim Rockford. I'm grateful to Mitch and Luigi in Albuquerque for embedding me into the methamphetamine world of *Breaking Bad*, and also to the three Mikes at Calibers Gun Club for keeping me safe.

To the lovely staff and friendly locals at Molly's Bar in NYC, Jack Melnik's Corner Tap in Chicago, Bamboula's in NOLA, Chez Jays in Santa Monica, Little Anita's in

Albuquerque and The Cowgirl in Santa Fe for making me feel at home.

Finally, my huge appreciation and love to all the amazing Amtrak employees I met along the way for looking after me so well.

Silver Streak

About the Author

Matthew Woodward is a rail-based adventurer and writer based in Chichester, West Sussex. Previously living and working in Edinburgh, he decided to quit the rat race after a successful career in drinks marketing. He now writes for a variety of publications on long-range rail travel. He is a Fellow of the Royal Geographical Society. *Silver Streak* is his fourth book.

For more information, please visit

www.matthew-woodward.com

Printed in Great Britain
by Amazon

73236868R00168